Creating Effective
Marketing Communications

Marketing in Action Series

Series Editor: Norman Hart

In producing this series, the advice and assistance has been sought of a prestigious editorial panel representing the principal professional bodies, trade associations and business schools.

The Series Editor for the Marketing in Action books is Norman Hart who is a writer of some ten books himself. He currently runs his own marketing consultancy, and is also an international lecturer at marketing and other such conferences as well as the leading business schools.

Creating Effective Marketing Communications

Daniel L Yadin

Series Editor: Norman Hart

KOGAN
PAGE

First published in 1994

Apart from any fair dealing for the purposes of research or private study, or criticism or review, as permitted under the Copyright, Designs and Patents Act, 1988, this publication may only be reproduced, stored or transmitted, in any form or by any means, with the prior permission in writing of the publishers, or in the case of reprographic reproduction in accordance with the terms of licences issued by the Copyright Licensing Agency. Enquiries concerning reproduction outside those terms should be sent to the publishers at the undermentioned address:

Kogan Page Limited
120 Pentonville Road
London N1 9JN

© Daniel L Yadin, 1994

British Library Cataloguing in Publication Data

A CIP record for this book is available from the British Library.

ISBN 0 7494 1208 9

Typeset by DP Photosetting, Aylesbury, Bucks
Printed and bound in Great Britain by
Biddles Ltd, Guildford and King's Lynn

Contents

PART 3   INFORMATION SOURCES

Introduction: A Practical Book for Practical Marketers

I first had the idea of writing this book while lecturing to management executives at the Chartered Institute of Marketing. Many delegates confided that copywriting and other creative tasks had been dumped on them at short notice – even though they had few skills to handle them.

This change now seems a permanent feature of marketing life; it is growing in other business areas as well.

I also offer this book to a generation of bright, enthusiastic CAM students. Because of changes in the CAM syllabus, they have lost a chance to glimpse the intriguing creative side of marketing and advertising. I hope they will pick up some of it here.

I am a pragmatic, professional copywriter, and put theory into practice every working day. Now that you have got your hands on this book, I hope you will keep it within reach. Read and re-read it, and put the thinking and techniques I have outlined into action.

WHAT THIS BOOK IS ABOUT

It offers you practical advice on creating effective marketing communications.

It is about applying the art of good salesmanship to the crafts of advertising and public relations.

Practical advice on creating effective marketing communications.

It is about seduction – the art of seducing your customer into changing his or her attitude in favour of your brand, product, service or ideas.

Above all, it is about proven techniques. In the publicity mix, you select different technique combinations for different marketing situations. Selecting which will work for your own marketing plans is up to you. The creative ammunition is in these pages.

WHO WILL BENEFIT

For both experienced marketers and those starting out.

Creating Effective Marketing Communications is both for experienced marketers striving for greater professionalism, and those starting out.

It is written particularly for directors, managers and executives responsible for:

❏ advertising
❏ brand management
❏ corporate communications
❏ direct mail
❏ exporting
❏ importing
❏ marketing
❏ marketing communications

❏ marketing training
❏ marketing services
❏ merchandising
❏ product management
❏ publicity
❏ sales
❏ sales management
❏ sales promotion.

Plus ...

❏ owners and managers of small businesses;
❏ directors and managers of charities, and non–profit organisations with small promotional budgets;
❏ advertising agency marketing departments;
❏ everyone using marketing communications to generate greater response and more sales.

However ...

Although it is not aimed specifically at:

❏ copywriters
❏ art directors
❏ designers

❏ print buyers
❏ art buyers
❏ advertising and print production specialists

... it is worthwhile having this book for consultation whenever the need arises. Which, judging by the current trend, will be often.

HOW TO USE THIS BOOK TO IMPROVE YOUR CREATIVE SKILLS

❏ Most chapters contain guidelines, the main points of a particular technique. This is a reference to use as an *aide-mémoire*.
❏ This is followed by a tutorial, point by point, based on the guidelines.

This simple format gives you the opportunity to study in detail a technique you are unfamiliar with. Later, when you need to refer quickly, just consult the guidelines.

THANKS

My thanks to Ruth Yadin for checking my manuscript, and to Martyn Davis for reading the proofs.

NOTE

Throughout this book, for the sake of brevity and simplicity, man embraces woman, so to speak; 'he' is used to include 'she'.

You will discover repetition of certain ideas, sentences and phrases in the text of the book. This is quite deliberate. It allows guidelines and explanatory copy to be presented complete and self-contained.

Brand names, personal names, addresses, telephone and fax numbers in the advertisement and script examples have been created especially for this book. They are solely for illustration purposes.

Part 1

Practical Planning Techniques

Chapter 1
Creative Planning Techniques

The problem with creative planning is that you always need it, but hardly ever have time to do it.

Inspiration sometimes does indeed come to marketing creatives, but is unreliable. Anyone who tells you that great campaigns are conceived in the bath is probably lying. To meet deadlines, you need something more professional, more structured and systematic.

Creative planning starts with the marketing plan. This is a comprehensive working document, detailing the marketing team's total approach for the forthcoming campaign. Examine it; familiarise yourself with its contents. Much of what is regarded as inspiration can be found within. With a bit of study, ideas can drop straight into your lap.

Creative planning starts with the marketing plan.

If the marketing team has done its job well – and they usually do – creative planning can save you time, as well as organise your creativity.

Creative planning can save you time.

Brand management is in the ideal position to analyse the marketing plan. A good brand manager will digest the plan, and abstract the elements needed for preparing integrated creative proposals. Agency account managers usually do this for their creative teams.

If you are in a marketing department and assigned a creative task, you should be able to lift out the creative elements from the marketing plan for yourself.

GUIDELINES

❑ At whom is the communication aimed?
❑ What are the media and delivery methods?
❑ What is the specific objective of the communication?
❑ What information is to be conveyed?
❑ What is the lead benefit?
❑ What satisfactions must be targeted?
❑ What are my recipient's expectations from this communication?
❑ How will I meet them?
❑ What response do I want from this communication?
❑ My communication objective will be achieved if my customer thinks, believes, or is convinced that...

Communications objectives.

EXPLOITING THESE TECHNIQUES

This is a *practical* checklist. It helps to organise your thinking for creative marketing communications, and acts as a model for evaluating the results.

It is not a substitute for thought. It is an essential aid to better organised planning, and faster, more accurate fulfilment of your communications objectives.

❑ At whom is the communication aimed?
You need to know and understand your target audience. For example: are your targets new users, existing users, or brand-switchers?

However, there may be a complex pass-along route for your proposition: initiators, specifiers, influencers, decision-takers, buyers, end-users. Each may need different treatment and motivations to push them over the edge; they may all have to agree, separately and together, on your proposition.

❑ What are the media and delivery methods?
The same thinking applies here. You also need to consider whether your communication is delivered via printed or broadcast media, by mail, or delivered by a salesman and left for further study and decision-making.

❑ What is the specific objective of the communication?

Is it, for example, to generate enquiries or sales leads, or to elicit money off the page? Decide here.

❑ What information is to be conveyed?

You need to list all the information needed for this communication, and arrange it in order of priority.

❑ What is the lead benefit?

Seek out the most important, practical or attractive selling point, which will motivate your customer most effectively. This is the one to lead with. Consider making this the subject of your headline and first paragraph of body copy.

❑ What satisfactions must be targeted? How will I meet them?

Consider what your target audience actually wants to hear or learn. If you are offering solutions to problems, make sure you feature them in your copy. For example: doctors in general practice certainly want to cure their patients, but they want empty waiting-rooms even more. If your product can help them to achieve this, make it clear; think about making it the lead benefit.

❑ What response do I want from this communication?

Is the appeal of your communication, and its leading ideas, powerful enough to make your customer do what you need to fulfil your objective: pick up the telephone and ask for a demonstration? call a credit-card hotline? fill in a coupon? visit a store or office? visit an exhibition? change their fixed ideas? take a decision in favour of your brand?

❑ My communication objective will be achieved if my customer thinks, believes or is convinced that . . .

This is the toughest of all the tasks in the chapter, but essential if you are to arrive at the correct message.

The easiest way is to write the answer out in full, using your customer's thoughts as your guide.

If you find it difficult to resolve right away, go back to your brief. Then handcuff yourself to your desk until you have completed the answer completely and honestly.

A tiny consolation: you are not alone here. I and many of my most experienced colleagues often find this task difficult. It does get a little easier with practice, however.

Chapter 2
Creative Briefings

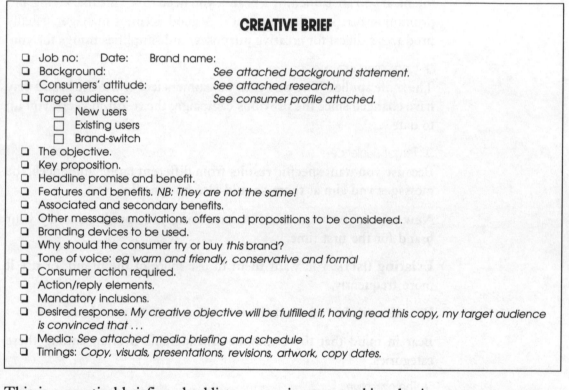

CREATIVE BRIEF

- ❏ Job no: Date: Brand name:
- ❏ Background: *See attached background statement.*
- ❏ Consumers' attitude: *See attached research.*
- ❏ Target audience: *See consumer profile attached.*
  - ☐ New users
  - ☐ Existing users
  - ☐ Brand-switch
- ❏ The objective.
- ❏ Key proposition.
- ❏ Headline promise and benefit.
- ❏ Features and benefits. *NB: They are not the same!*
- ❏ Associated and secondary benefits.
- ❏ Other messages, motivations, offers and propositions to be considered.
- ❏ Branding devices to be used.
- ❏ Why should the consumer try or buy *this* brand?
- ❏ Tone of voice: *eg warm and friendly, conservative and formal*
- ❏ Consumer action required.
- ❏ Action/reply elements.
- ❏ Mandatory inclusions.
- ❏ Desired response. *My creative objective will be fulfilled if, having read this copy, my target audience is convinced that ...*
- ❏ Media: *See attached media briefing and schedule*
- ❏ Timings: *Copy, visuals, presentations, revisions, artwork, copy dates.*

This is a practical briefing checklist; we use it every working day in our own business. It is not a substitute for thought, but an aid to better organised creative thinking. An essential discipline for briefing your colleagues, it also helps to discipline those briefing *you*.

This is a practical briefing checklist.

It helps you to arrive at the *correct* messages, which you can hone to perfection, and avoid wasting time on incorrect ones.

It helps you arrive at the correct messages.

This is just about the minimum you need for getting started on your next piece of copy. You will certainly be adding practical elements of your own – using your professional experience to guide you. In other words, the hard way.

❏ Date, job number and brand

If you have several jobs running at the same time, you *must* have a clear system of identification. If you haven't, set one up now.

❏ Background

There should always be a background statement available. This can range from the complete history of the brand to a simple statement of intent. If you are launching a brand, you need to see the marketing and promotion briefs in their entirety. A good account manager usually produces a digest for creative purposes, and simplifies things for you.

❏ Consumers' attitude

The same applies. The way your consumers feel or use the brand may have changed since the previous campaign; the research keeps you up to date.

❏ Target audience

Because you want specific results from different target audiences, the messages you aim at them should also be specific.

New users: you want them to start using your product, to try your brand for the first time.

Existing users: you want them to use more of the brand, or use it more frequently.

Brand-switch: you want them to come over to your brand.

Bear in mind that there may be considerable overlap among these categories.

❏ The objective

1. The objective of the campaign, clearly stated in terms you can use.
2. Answer these questions:
   - What precisely does this advertisement, mailer or brochure have to achieve?
   - What response must the copy produce?

❏ Key proposition

Decide on the *lead benefit*: the single, strongest, most important sales point in the whole brief which will best motivate your reader, viewer or listener.

❑ Headline promise and benefit

The major sales point you have decided on now needs to be written as a persuasive headline. You may need to consider using a sub-headline as well. Remember to link your first line, sentence and paragraph of body copy to it.

❑ Features and benefits

The features and facts you are promoting are what your product does; the benefits are what your product does *for your customer!*

In copy, features and benefits should always be locked together. Sometimes it is best to show only the benefits. This applies especially when space and time are restricted. Whatever you decide, every consumer benefit must have a feature behind it.

❑ Associated and secondary benefits

Guarantees, warranties and other benefits which do not form part of your main persuasion, but nevertheless reward the reader for deciding on your brand.

❑ Branding devices to be used

If your product has a strong branding device, strive to build it in to your headline copy. Look at Coca Cola, Castlemain XXXX, and other strong branders in today's media.

❑ Why should the consumer try or buy *this* brand?

In copywriting, intellectual honesty is greater than absolute truth. Examine what you have written and designed. If you can see the answer to this question in it, you have succeeded. If you cannot, start again.

❑ Tone of voice

Tailor the technique to the target. Decide which effect you want to achieve, relative to the target audience and its needs.

❑ Consumer action required

Decide exactly what you want your reader, viewer and listener to do after absorbing your message.

❑ Action/reply elements

Choose the elements which maximise it most efficiently. Consider coupon, freepost, telephone, freefone, 0800, 0345, fax – and the other reply tools at your disposal.

❑ Mandatory inclusions

Space and air-time is always limited, so you need to reserve room for mandatories in your copy. Financial, tobacco and medical products have specific mandatories. Don't forget logos, straplines and campaign slogans.

❑ Desired response

This is the final test of your ability to drive the message home and get the response you want. Complete the sentence; be honest about it.

❑ Media

The media schedule will give you a great deal of information about your target audience. Insist on seeing the schedule, and the research data that goes with it.

❑ Timings

Time is not elastic. Make sure you have enough time to complete your assignment. If not, you may have to work at night. Don't we all?

GETTING AND GIVING A CREATIVE BRIEFING

Treat creatives like the professionals they are.

Creatives are specialists. Like you, they are professionals; they deserve to be treated in a professional way.

❑ Always give a clear brief.
❑ Before every briefing, make up your mind what you want.
❑ Don't mess them about. Don't keep on changing your mind.
❑ Be prepared to take advice. Creatives know their jobs as well as you do yours. They should be *encouraged* to make a contribution.
❑ Insist on work of the highest quality; make it clear that this is what you are buying.
❑ Get a reputation for paying promptly. It's amazing how the most skilled creatives tend to gravitate to your office.

Make these guidelines work for you.

When you are receiving a briefing from your boss, colleagues or other non-creatives, make sure you get these guidelines working for you.

Part 2

Improving Your Creative Skills

Chapter 3
Copywriting Techniques for Sales-winning Ads and Print

By this time, you should have looked at the promotional plan for the campaign you are going to create. You will also have acquired all the information you need.

Where you are so far.

You will have set your communications objectives using the checklist in Chapter 1, and gone through the creative briefing session, using the checklist in Chapter 2.

You will have identified your target audience, and decided on your copy platform – what you need to say.

What you need now is to start writing and designing. For that, you use another essential tool: a creative discipline.

There are several well-known techniques. One we use very successfully is AIDA. If you have ever been a sales rep, you will recognise this as a discipline of *progressive steps* in the process of making a sale.

AIDA is a communication discipline, an intellectual tool which helps you to achieve:

AIDA is a communication discipline.

1. The levels of understanding *you* need for writing effective copy;
2. The level of understanding you want *your target audience* to achieve, to give you the response you want.

AIDA is an acronym for:

Attention
Interest
Desire
Action.

This is a logical progression, and applies to all marketing communications:

❑ You must first grab your reader's attention.
❑ Tell him something that appeals to his self-interest.
❑ Arouse a strong desire to try, buy or examine your product, to send for your literature or to ask for a sales call.
❑ Urge your reader into taking the action you want.

You may feel that this technique is too basic. However, if you want to enjoy caviare and champagne, you should start with meat and boiled potatoes. If you really want to sharpen your creative skills, and do it quickly and reliably, you need to practise basics which are both proven and reliable.

Practise the basics to sharpen your creative skills.

GRABBING ATTENTION

How to grab attention: make a strong promise.

Your attention-grabber must do the job in a single glance, otherwise you lose your reader. You must therefore make a promise strong enough to reach off the page and grab your reader by the eyeballs.

In writing a press advertisement, your objective should be to entice your reader to *read on*.

For TV and radio commercials, you must get your viewer to pay attention, and *continue looking or listening*. Given the transient nature of these media, this is a tough task.

Writing a brochure, your primary objective is to get the reader to *open the first page*, and discover what the proposition is going to do for him.

AROUSING INTEREST

Three important criteria.

When producing advertisements and print, your creative work must fulfil three important criteria:

For sales-winning videos that grab your customers by the eyeballs

Need something special for sales presentations? Call us now.
We'll make you outstanding videos that really
win sales and influence buyers.

Telephone Creative Director Martin Jones for a discussion and a showreel:
082 090 0550, or fax 082 090 0506

VIDEO DYNAMICS

Dynamics House, Alban Street, London NW1 4VD

Does the visual attract attention? Is there a promise in the headline? Is the copy benefit-led? Are the contact numbers bold enough?

❏ It must *be interesting* to the reader;
❏ It must *look* interesting;
❏ It must be *easy to read and understand.*

Appeal to self-interest – the magic ingredient.

To be interesting, your copy must appeal to your reader's self-interest – the magic ingredient.

❏ Copy must be specific, full of interesting benefits, facts and features, preferably linked together. Avoid generalisations – they turn your reader off.
❏ Make your copy lively. Your reader won't take boring copy, however short it is. He may read quite long copy if it is interesting enough.
❏ When editing your copy, purge the generalisations and leave the benefits and facts intact.
❏ Use words like 'you' and 'yours'. It's a way of assuring your reader that you understand him, his needs, problems and aspirations.

MAKING COPY LOOK INTERESTING

How to make your copy look interesting.

❏ Break your copy into short, easy-to-understand paragraphs. Don't make them too short; it looks messy.
❏ Vary the length.
❏ Limit each paragraph to two or three related ideas.
❏ Punctuate your copy with subheads and cross-heads. They encourage your customer to read on. It makes it easier to get into the copy at any point that offers immediate appeal. Don't think your reader will go through your copy from end to end – he won't.
❏ Use typographical devices; they help to make copy readable and encourage the customer to read on. For more, see Chapter 13.

MAKING COPY EASY TO UNDERSTAND

How to make your copy easy to understand.

❏ Short sentences are usually easier to assimilate than long ones. Don't put more than one idea into a sentence.

Be reasonable about the length of sentences; don't tax your reader's concentration.

As a general rule, if there are more than two commas in the sentence you have just written, it's too long. Vary the length.

❑ Use simple words and phrases. Ordinary consumers and professionals can be swayed by strong, well-reasoned arguments, simply expressed.

❑ Paragraph length: similar principles apply.

AROUSING THE READER'S DESIRE

You need to do more than just create a desire for your brand.

More than creating a desire is required.

❑ Before action comes decision. You must aim to get your reader to make *a decision in favour of your brand*.

❑ Your aim should be to arouse an avid desire, an eagerness, an impatience to possess it, examine it, get a demonstration.

❑ To do this, you should implant the idea of using your product and benefiting from it. Generate the euphoria of owning it – remembering, of course, to avoid mentioning the pain of paying for it.

❑ Make sure it's *your* brand the reader desires. Create a preference for it above all others. Don't sell other brands by implication, or by using generalisations.

To get a preference for your brand:

❑ distinguish it from all others;

❑ show your customer why it's so good for him;

❑ get him to agree it's the only one that's good for him.

GETTING THE ACTION YOU WANT

This, of course, is what you have been working towards all along. It follows that you should strive to make the utmost of the space you have for the reply element.

Make the most of the space for the reply element.

You should have your reader on a 'high' at this point. Now read the Guidelines on the next page.

GUIDELINES

- ❑ Put a promise in the headline.
- ❑ Make it a benefit; offer a solution.
- ❑ Appeal to your customer's self-interest.
- ❑ Write visually. Arouse visual images in your reader's mind.
- ❑ Use strong branding. Bolt your idea and the brand name firmly together.
- ❑ The first sentence of your body copy should link straight into your headline.
- ❑ Begin with a fact, not a generalisation; go for the jugular.
- ❑ Use benefits, not facts alone.
- ❑ Remember: what you are selling may not be what your customer is buying.
- ❑ Be persuasive.
- ❑ Get your customer involved. Use 'you' frequently.
- ❑ Keep copy terse. Make paragraphs and sentences short but readable.
- ❑ Use subheads to guide your reader through the copy.
- ❑ Avoid long words where short ones do the same job.
- ❑ Talk your customer's everyday language.
- ❑ 'The more you tell, the more you sell.' Who wrote that?
- ❑ Urge your customer to take the action *you* want.
- ❑ Use as much persuasion in the reply element as in the rest of the advertisement.
- ❑ Show your customer it's *in his interest* to respond to your proposition.
- ❑ Demonstrate *the benefits* that come from responding.
- ❑ Make it *worthwhile* to respond – offer an incentive.
- ❑ Show clearly *how* to respond.
- ❑ Make it *as easy as possible* to take action.
- ❑ Tell him *to do it*, and to take the action *now*.

EXPLOITING THESE TECHNIQUES

❑ Put a promise in the headline

The question you have to address is the one going through the customer's mind when he sees your headline:

'What's in it for me? If nothing, why should I bother to read on?'

This thought may not be expressed only in words, but also in the abstract. Either way, if your reader can't see immediately what the promise is, there's nothing to hold his attention. After that, nothing will encourage him to read the rest of your copy.

Most people are exposed to over 1500 promotional messages every day. You see how vital it is to get your headline and its promise noticed and understood. The rest of your copy depends on it.

❑ Make it a benefit; offer a solution

Because life is full of problems, everybody is looking for solutions.

People want solutions to their domestic, personal, physical, medical, business and financial problems.

If you can offer solutions to your readers' problems, you're in business! When your headline shows that your product or service promises such solutions, you can rely on their rapt attention and sustained interest.

❑ Appeal to your customer's self-interest

Most people act in their own self-interest, either instinctively, out of habit, or after careful consideration. You can rely on it, so write your copy to appeal to it.

❑ Write visually

Writing abstract copy is sometimes unavoidable.

Next time you write an abstract line, think about how your art director will handle it. His job is getting your copy onto a layout pad. I'm sure you've seen art directors struggling with abstractions; have you felt their desperation?

❑ Use strong branding

Research suggests that sometimes people see an advertising message and unconsciously substitute their favourite brand name for the one in the message. It seems they do this even when the message content appeals to them very much.

Aim to avoid this. Make your branding work persuasively with the creative idea you are using.

❑ Link the body copy with your headline

If your headline is doing its job, and arousing your reader's expectations, he will look for them to be fulfilled at once. Don't keep him hanging about for the fulfilment. Put it in the first sentence of the body copy.

❑ Get your customer involved

Every customer, every reader, viewer and listener, is an individual. Each has individual needs, so make sure your copy helps to fulfil them. By using personal words, you can get your customer more involved in understanding your offer and its personal value.

❑ Keep copy terse

'Terse' doesn't mean 'short'; it means 'tight'.

Redundant words and phrases can slow down your message, and also give an amateurish feel to your copy. If that's what you want, fine. Otherwise purge redundant words carefully but ruthlessly. Effective, creative copy depends as much on efficient editing as on careful planning.

❑ Use subheads

Plan to write paragraphs that contain related ideas which group together logically. Subheads signal what is coming, and should be both logical and informative. They help both to guide the reader through the copy, and encourage those who like to skim before reading everything.

❑ Avoid long words

Where a short word does the same job as a long one, use it. This makes your text easier to read and understand.

❑ Use everyday language

The language you use in copywriting should be your customer's, not your own. Think about the language of his geographical area, occupation, age, social group. Think about his needs and problems.

❑ What you are selling – and what your customer is buying

You may be selling electric irons – electro-mechanical hardware. But your customer will be buying the ability to impress an employer, a supplier, or a member of the opposite sex. Think about his *motives*.

❑ Use benefits, not facts alone

You can make facts and product features work more persuasively when you bolt them together with the benefits they bring to your customer. In copy, always harness them together.

❑ 'The more you tell, the more you sell'

Hardly anybody today remembers Claude Hopkins. He invented test marketing, copy testing and brand research. David Ogilvy says that nobody should be allowed to go near advertising until he has read Claude Hopkins' book seven times. I agree. And this book too.

❑ Urge your customer to take the action you want

Be specific. Feature the response element boldly and visibly – even dramatically. It could increase your response level.

This decision is based on the most efficient method of getting the response, how easy it is for your customer to respond, and how fast and efficiently your company can handle the response you generate.

You can get action off the page, off the screen or off air by using:

- ❏ coupons
- ❏ telephone numbers
- ❏ order forms
- ❏ credit card hotline
- ❏ outlet addresses
- ❏ reply cards.

For sales-winning videos
to knock your customers' socks off...
call
VIDEO DYNAMICS

Need something really *special* for sales presentations? Get Video Dynamics to make your videos.

With our experience and creative expertise behind you, you'll make a great deal more than just a good impression on your customers. You'll make an outstanding one that wins sales and influences buyers!

We analyse your objectives, research your needs, find the solutions, stick to your budget and deliver on time.

Want to know more? Telephone our Creative Director Martin Jones now for advice (no obligation), and our dynamic showreel, on

082 090 0505, or fax him on **082 090 0506**

VIDEO DYNAMICS
Dynamics House, Alban Street, London NW1 4VD

Is there a promise in the headline? Does it go through AIDA? Is the copy benefit-led? Is the writing terse, active? Is the response element visible?

❏ Use as much persuasion in the reply element as in the rest of the advertisement
Every coupon and reply card you write should be a mini-ad in itself: a persuasive headline, short, benefit-led copy, campaign slogan, strong branding.

❏ Show your customer it's in his interest to respond
Tempt your customer into action – offer an incentive wherever possible. Use facts and benefits persuasively, and your customer will be seduced into listening to your propositions.

❏ Make it worthwhile to respond - offer an incentive
A discount, a free gift, a special pack, three for the price of two – the incentive can be quite modest.

❏ Demonstrate the benefits that come from responding
Your customer will take your proposition seriously when you show how he benefits from responding. Use images as well as words.

❏ Show clearly how to respond
Design and write coupons with the reader in mind. Allow adequate space for the information you want. Put it in words. For example: 'Fill in your initials, surname, job title and company address'. This also helps you build viable databases. If you are featuring a telephone number, *really* feature it – make it big and bold and visible.

❏ Make it as easy as possible to take action
You can make it easy to respond by using:

❏ Freepost   ❏ 0800 numbers
❏ reply-paid envelopes   ❏ 0345 numbers
❏ Freephone.

Give the customer a name to ask for when he telephones for information. This can prevent a breakdown of the enquiry at the switchboard, and channel your customer direct to the right person without delay.

❏ Tell him to do it, and to take the action now
Put a time limit on your offer. Add an extra benefit if he responds within the limit, and you have a powerful incentive for action.

A word of warning: if a prospective customer puts your coupon under the mantelpiece clock, for attention after tea, you may never see it again. Likewise, the 'pending' or 'action' tray is a graveyard.

Chapter 4

How to Write Effective Headlines

What makes a headline effective? It depends who you are.

If you are a product manager, it is a promotion device that helps to sell your brand. If you are a marketing director, an effective headline is something that helps to move crates of product out of your factory at high speed. As a company accountant, you may regard a headline as something that helps to swell your bottom line.

What makes an effective headline?

On the other hand, when you are a copywriter, an effective headline is a piece of well-crafted, motivating text. It sits on top of your advertisement, reaches off the page and grabs readers by the eyeballs. It helps to drive your prospective customers into making decisions in favour of your brand.

If you are a prospective customer, is it something you see in a magazine that prompts you to think 'I like that; I'll try it?'

There is more controversy over headlines than almost any other aspect of marketing communications. For example, I have had marketing managers on copywriting courses waver over really excellent headlines, on the grounds of length or of brevity.

I have had really motivating headlines rejected by clients because of full-stops at the ends.

Some people, David Ogilvy among them, feel that headlines should not print reversed white out of black. Others, that headlines should not be set in caps, since this impedes readability.

Whatever your own problems with headlines, this chapter will give you practical guidelines on resolving them.

Practical guidelines for improving headlines.

Having a birthday?
Bring out the Sunshine!

Sunshine Margarine brings out the very best in your
baking. Gives heavenly texture and taste to
everything you touch. For cakes with child-appeal.
Brilliant biscuits. Perfect pies.

Put golden Sunshine on your shopping list now. Even
if it's not your birthday, you'll love the taste.
And so will your guests.

☼ SUNSHINE
That heavenly taste

Peckish?
Bring out the Sunshine

Reach for the Sunshine Margarine, everybody's
favourite taste. Spreads like a dream - straight from
the fridge, so there's no waiting for for a snack to
relieve the pangs.

Put golden Sunshine on your shopping list now. Even
if you're not absolutely ravenous, that heavenly taste
will keep you going till dinner-time.

☼ SUNSHINE
That heavenly taste

Same brand, different target audiences. Are these advertisements aimed at new users, existing
users or brand-switchers?

GUIDELINES

- ❑ Put a promise into your headline. Make it an important consumer benefit.
- ❑ Use strong branding.
- ❑ Differentiate your brand. Show its uniqueness.
- ❑ Use positive propositions. Offer solutions.
- ❑ Appeal to your reader's self-interest. Talk his language.
- ❑ Make your headlines relevant.
- ❑ Never use wit for its own sake.
- ❑ Don't exaggerate. Avoid superlatives, unless they do a real job.
- ❑ Write visually. Arouse visual images in your reader's mind.
- ❑ Use trigger-words, emotive words, interesting words, motivating words.
- ❑ Avoid long words where short ones do the same job.
- ❑ Keep headlines terse.
- ❑ Entice. Seduce. Aim to urge the customer to read on. Use 'you' frequently.
- ❑ Get your reader involved.

EXPLOITING THESE TECHNIQUES

❑ Put a promise into your headline

David Ogilvy, one of the world's successful copywriters, has some illuminating things to say about headlines.*

On average, he claims, five times as many people read headlines as read body copy. It follows that, when you have created your headline, you have committed eighty pence of your promotional pound. If you haven't fired your best selling shot in your headline, you have probably wasted 80 per cent of your money.

Read again what I have said about this in Chapter 3.

❑ Use strong branding

Lock the creative idea in the headline with your brand name or other brand property. Make them work together, and your reader will identify them as one, and the benefit you are offering as well.

❑ Differentiate your brand

If your brand faces competition, make sure your reader knows the difference, clearly expressed in the main benefit.

---

* Ogilvy, D., *Confessions of an Advertising Man* (1962), Atheneum, New York.

FRESHAIR
air purifiers

For greater comfort, protection and productivity at work

Installing 👍Freshair air purifiers does much more than improve the atmosphere in your office, boardroom, meeting rooms and canteen.

RESTORES AIR FRESHNESS

👍Improves your working environment by constantly

restoring air freshness all over your office. 👍Helps your staff to work more comfortably; helps raise their productivity and morale.

CUTS DOWN TOBACCO SMOKE, DUST AND POLLEN

👍Helps to prolong the working life of your equipment by protecting against dust build-up and nicotine

corrosion. 👍Helps all your staff to work more comfortably and productively - especially non-smokers and hay-fever sufferers.

REDUCES STATIC BUILD-UP

👍Helps to protect your sensitive equipment and magnetic media from irreversible damage.

Get a demonstration of 👍Freshair air purifiers in your own office. For a demo, a discussion or an information pack, please telephone Derek Smyth on 082 090 0505, or fax him on 090 0506.

👍 *FRESHAIR*
Freshair House, Alban Row, London NW1 4FR

There is a promise in the headline; features and user-benefits march together. Using Derek Smyth's name in the action line directs enquiries to someone who knows about the product and the solutions it offers.

❏ Use positive propositions

If you really need to highlight a problem your reader has, offer the solution at the same time, and base it on your brand.

❏ Appeal to your reader's self-interest

If you don't, why should he bother to read it? See what I have said in Chapter 3 about this.

❏ Make your headlines relevant

Relevant to what? To your reader's self-interest. And, of course, to what you are selling – to your brand.

❏ Never use wit for its own sake

Humour is a minefield. But a joke is hard to ignore – you either love or hate it. Its practical use is getting your reader involved with your proposition.

❏ Don't exaggerate

Be careful with words like 'amazing', 'fantastic' and 'incredible'. They won't do a proper job unless they are part of a thoroughly believable proposition.

❏ Write visually

Especially if your headline is abstract. You need to plant strong images in your reader's mind. Give your art director a fair chance to get your idea on paper. Consult before you write!

❏ Use trigger-words

What's a trigger-word? One which propels your reader into your proposition, towards the action you want. Examples: *free*, *new*, *opportunity*, *guarantee*, *service*, *love*, *save*, *value*, *extra*. Be careful: your words must be relevant to your target.

❏ Avoid long words where short ones do the same job

Talk your reader's everyday language. Where you must use jargon, try to use common language for persuasion.

❏ Keep headlines terse

Terse does not mean short. It means tight. Purge redundant words and phrases. A headline can be any length, provided that every word pays its way.

❏ Entice, seduce

You cannot *make* your reader do anything. But you can attract, entice and persuade. Again, tailor the technique to the target.

❏ Get your reader involved

Don't write a headline as though it were aimed at an anonymous third party. If you want to influence your reader, talk direct to that reader. Use words like *you, yours, yourself, your company, your home.*

Chapter 5

How to Write Effective Body Copy

GUIDELINES

- ❏ Your first sentence and paragraph should link into your headline.
- ❏ If your headline asks a question, supply the answer immediately.
- ❏ Appeal to your customer's self-interest.
- ❏ Use benefits as well as facts and features.
- ❏ Maintain the strength of the branding theme.
- ❏ Make ideas and sentences flow logically into each other.
- ❏ Use your reader's language.
- ❏ Write with clarity; aim to persuade.
- ❏ Keep copy terse. Don't waste words.
- ❏ Avoid repetition, except for emphasis.
- ❏ Use short words, unless long ones achieve more impact and authority.
- ❏ Use subheads, cross-heads, italics, bold, small caps and other typographical devices.
- ❏ Use sentences to separate ideas; use paragraphing to keep similar ideas together.
- ❏ Urge the customer to respond actively.

EXPLOITING THESE TECHNIQUES

❏ Link into your headline

Your reader will not wait to make the connection; therefore, get straight into it.

❏ If your headline asks a question, supply the answer immediately

The same applies. What's more, if you don't supply an answer, in whatever form, your reader may feel cheated, and could turn to another brand in revenge. The answer, therefore, *must* be a consumer or business benefit.

❏ Appeal to your customer's self-interest

Again, the magic ingredient. You cannot expect him to read what you have written unless you continue the relevance you have created.

❏ Use benefits as well as facts

Lock them together – side by side, if you can, especially if your research tells you that the customer likes substantiation. In any case, you should not create a benefit without having a fact to support it. And vice versa.

❏ Maintain the strength of the branding theme

You can actually build up the impact of your branding in body copy. Aim to leave your reader even better disposed towards your brand than when he started reading.

❏ Make ideas and sentences flow logically

If your copy jumps around, your reader gets confused. What do readers tend to do when confused? Nothing. And that's definitely not what you want.

❏ Use your reader's language

Your readers or viewers may not talk the way you do. Study how *they* speak, what style they most easily absorb and understand. The way to do this is to study the media they are exposed to. If you can't spare the time to go to Aberdeen and listen to the way people speak there, read their local paper.

❏ Write with clarity; aim to persuade

Use the benefits and facts at your disposal and use them persuasively. Be direct about it. You have to make a conscious decision to do this before you begin writing. It's not easy, but you must do it.

❏ Keep copy terse. Don't waste words

Terse does not mean 'short'. It means tight, concise and smooth-flowing. Purge all redundant words and phrases from your copy.

❏ Avoid repetition

Some arguments and copywriting styles benefit from repetition. It helps to convey emphasis, credibility and authority. However, try not to use exactly the same words the second time round. And don't overdo it.

❏ Use short words

I am *not* saying that short words are best under all circumstances. But that's the way most people speak. Tailor the technique to the target; as always, use your judgement.

❏ Use subheads, cross-heads, italics, bold, small caps and other typographical devices

Use them to separate major ideas from one another; it makes your copy easier to read and understand. Equally important, they enhance the visual impact of your body copy – make it *look* more interesting, which encourages your customer *to start reading*.

For specific techniques which help you, see Chapter 13.

❏ Using sentences and paragraphs

They have specific uses in copywriting. Read Chapter 13 for specific techniques.

❏ Urge the customer to respond actively

Show the customer that it is *worthwhile* to respond; demonstrate all the benefits that come from responding. Then tell him to do it, to act *right* away: pick up the phone and ask for information, a brochure or a sales call; phone your credit card hotline; send a fax; fill in and post the coupon. If the action you want is physical, ask for it.

Remember the rep's dictum: *Never leave without asking for the order!*

Chapter 6
Writing Effective Direct Mail

Direct mail as a means of personal communication.

Because direct mail is so selective, you can use it as a method of *personal communication*. In this way, you take full advantage of the directness and intimacy the medium offers.

You are able to control almost everything involved in a mail-shot. For example:

Colour	Envelope	Size
Content	Frequency	Stamping
Contents	Mailing list	Timing
Copy	Production technique	Typography
Creativity	Reply element	Volume
Design	Samples	Weight

There are few creative limitations. There are no limits to copy length, no restrictions on design, beyond those relating to legality, honesty and decency.

Basic principles of creating direct mail.

In creating sales letters, leaflets and brochures, the same basic principles apply as for press advertisements.

❏ Grab your reader's attention.
❏ Get him to turn the first page.
❏ Show how your brand is of benefit to him.
❏ Arouse a desire to try it, buy it or own it.
❏ Get action.

If a brochure you are creating is going to be sent out cold, that is almost certainly the reaction you will get: the cold shoulder. Waste-bins all over Britain are full of unsolicited mail!

On the other hand, sending a skilfully written letter with your brochure tempts your recipient with a personal message. It could exert a powerful, positive influence on the response you get.

A powerful and positive influence.

GUIDELINES

Effective sales letters

❑ Start with a headline. Put a promise or benefit into it.
❑ Make the promise personal.
❑ Address your reader by name in the salutation, and in the body copy.
❑ In a business mailing, use the recipient's job title.
❑ Try not to use 'Dear Sir or Madam'.
❑ Your first paragraph of body copy should link into the headline.
❑ If your headline is a question, make sure you supply the answer immediately in the body copy.
❑ Ensure your questions are open-ended.
❑ Make your copy easy to read – use typographical devices and colour.
❑ Keep copy terse.
❑ Body copy should be just long enough to cover facts, benefits and persuasion.
❑ Urge your reader to take action.
❑ Sign it.
❑ Use a PS as a clincher.
❑ Make it easy for your reader to reply.
❑ Put a persuasive sales message into the reply element.

EXPLOITING THESE TECHNIQUES

❑ Start with a headline. Put a promise or benefit into it
Make sure your reader knows, without a shadow of doubt, what's on offer. Put your key benefit here. Be persuasive. Use AIDA.

❑ Make the promise personal
Your letter is a personal communication. Make your promise a direct, personal benefit. Tailor the copy to the target.

❑ Address your reader by name in the salutation, and in the body copy
Make sure your mailing house gets it right. Ensure your in-house lists do.

❑ In a business mailing, use the recipient's job title
Again, your mailing house should be up-to-date enough to ensure accuracy; otherwise it can prejudice the response.

❑ Try not to use 'Dear Sir or Madam'

I am not needlessly condemning this salutation, of course. Some companies with extensive mail-order lists get a good response with it; others have no choice but to use it. One delegate on a recent CIM Print course had no alternative, and was getting worthwhile results from a huge consumer list. However, where there are alternatives, use and test them systematically.

Note: it is *not* compulsory to use a salutation in a sales letter. Try a couple of hundred copies of your next letter without one, and compare the results.

❑ Your first paragraph of body copy should link into the headline

Don't waste your reader's time easing yourself into the copy. As with press ads, get straight to the point.

❑ If your headline is a question, make sure you supply the answer immediately in the body copy

If you bury the answer in the body of your letter, your reader won't wait to get to it. Your letter will be binned.

❑ Ensure your questions are open-ended

Make sure the answer you are seeking is not a straight 'no'. If it is, the communication with your reader could end right there. Then where do you go?

❑ Make your copy easy to read - use typographical devices and colour

Use cross-heads, bold type, underlining, colour. Add *visual* variety to your copy. See Chapter 13.

❑ Keep copy terse

Terse does not mean 'short'; it means 'tight'. As with press ads, purge unnecessary words and phrases, avoid clichés and generalisations. Make every word pay its way. Your aim should be easier reading and better comprehension. Don't overdo the purging; copy can look eccentric, and also be difficult to read.

❑ Body copy should be just long enough to cover facts, benefits and persuasion

When you have grabbed your reader's attention and aroused his interest, hold that interest with important benefits and facts. Show how they give the satisfactions and solutions he is seeking.

If your sales letter turns out shorter than you expected, do not be tempted into padding it for the sake of length. If you use repetition, do so deliberately and with a specific objective; repeating an important offer, for example, could increase awareness at the end of a four-page letter.

If you can't get your sales pitch across in four or five paragraphs, consider creating a leaflet that tells the complete story.

❏ Urge your reader to take action

Try putting action copy in more than one place in the letter – in the second paragraph, for example, as well as at the end. The reason: if you can get your reader to agree to take action even *before* he has read the whole text, you have him on your side at the end too.

❏ Sign it

Even though you may not have begun with a salutation, a signature at the foot of a sales letter is a friendly way to end. It is also a convention, which most people are used to. Not all signatures are legible, so have the writer's name typed beneath it.

❏ Use a PS as a clincher

The postscript achieves high readership, while taking little space, so don't waste this opportunity to persuade.

There are several ways a PS can be useful: reinforcing a major offer; bringing out a minor point already made in body copy; introducing a new benefit, which might have been overlooked in body copy; introducing the closing date of an offer.

If you are repeating a point here, write it in a different way; don't make it a straight repeat.

❏ Make it easy for your reader to reply

Highlight the reply element; give it as much space as possible. If it is a telephone number, make it large enough to be really visible. If your reply element is a coupon, don't hide it away on a back page; if it is a reply card, feature it within the body copy.

Design every coupon and card with the reader in mind – make everything clear, with adequate space for first name, initials, surname, job title, company name, address. Include tick-boxes for information options.

❑ Put a persuasive sales message into the reply element

Write every coupon and reply card as a *persuasive advertisement*; make it pay its way! Give it a benefit-led headline and a line of body copy; illustrate the offer, sample or information pack. Do everything you can to *maximise* the response.

Chapter 7
Improving Your Brochures and Leaflets

GUIDELINES

General

- ❏ Aim to make every brochure you produce informative, motivating, attractive.
- ❏ Aim to make them interesting, look interesting, easy to read and understand.
- ❏ Aim to demonstrate how your brand works for your reader's benefit and self-interest.
- ❏ Aim to show your brand in action.
- ❏ Aim to arouse in your reader a desire to try, buy or possess or learn about your brand.
- ❏ Aim to demonstrate by example.

Front cover

- ❏ Grab your reader's attention.
- ❏ Aim to get the front cover opened – make this your primary objective.
- ❏ Make a promise; show a benefit.
- ❏ Propel your reader into the inside pages.

Inside pages

- ❏ Write a headline which links direct to the promise on the front cover.
- ❏ Use AIDA.
- ❏ As always, tailor the technique to the target.
- ❏ Ensure that your copy and design flow logically to the conclusion you want.
- ❏ Ensure your copy is easy to read and understand.
- ❏ Use subheads and cross-heads.
- ❏ Vary sentence and paragraph length.
- ❏ Use visual devices.
- ❏ For emphasis, use bold type, italics, underlining, small caps, colour.
- ❏ Use typography creatively, but not eccentrically.
- ❏ Don't use too many typefaces, weights and sizes.
- ❏ Make the design look busy, attractive, interesting, but never at the expense of clarity.
- ❏ When using a six-page format, make the most effective use of page 5.

> ### *Reply element*
>
> ❏ Make it visible.
> ❏ Write and design it as a promotion in its own right.
> ❏ Give it a headline; put a promise into it.
> ❏ Give it its own body copy, pay-off and action line.
> ❏ Make it interesting, look interesting, easy to read and understand.
> ❏ If possible, make it self-addressed; ensure the accuracy of the information.

EXPLOITING THESE TECHNIQUES

Front cover

❏ Grab your reader's attention

As with other forms of promotion, your opening idea must be strong enough to reach off the page and grab your reader by the eyeballs! Look at the key proposition, and find ways of basing your opening idea on that.

❏ Aim to get the front cover opened – make this your primary objective

If you can't do this, your entire effort fails. Tempt, seduce, intrigue, tease. Merely having the name of your company or brand name on the front page is just not good enough.

❏ Make a promise; show a benefit

Appeal to your reader's self-interest. If you have a solution to your reader's technical, corporate, domestic or personal problems, feature it here.

❏ Propel your reader into the inside pages

This is where you aim to do the main selling job on your customer. It amounts to nothing if you don't get your reader beyond the cover.

Inside pages

❏ Write a headline which links direct to the promise on the front cover

Justify, explain and expand your front cover proposition. Start with a headline which you can develop in the body copy.

❏ Use AIDA

Even within the body of a brochure or leaflet, you need to attract your reader's attention, generate interest, get a decision and encourage action. Scattering these elements too widely, however, makes pages look messy. Use your judgement.

For AIDA technique, see Chapter 3.

❏ As always, tailor the technique to the target

Bear in mind your reader's profession, occupation, education and location, and the language he uses. I once wrote a campaign for a retail outlet in Scotland. The client ticked me off with the words 'They don't talk like that in Glasgow!' Rebuked, I revised at once.

❏ Ensure that your copy and design flow logically to the conclusion you want

AIDA is an excellent tool to use for this. Construct the whole production with action in mind. If you want an active response to your mailshot, sit down with your art director and plan it that way. Designers use AIDA for the same reason you do, but sometimes they need to be coaxed.

❏ Ensure your copy is easy to read and understand

Don't expect your reader to assimilate large chunks of copy, unrelieved by adequate punctuation and typography. See Chapter 13 for guidelines.

❏ Use subheads and cross-heads

These are signposts, to guide your reader through the copy in the way you have planned. Face it: *nobody* is going to read your copy from the first word to the last. But you can tempt him to look for the things that interest him most. If he likes what he sees, he may read all the interesting bits, and then take action. Therefore, make sure each of your subheads and cross-heads is tempting, and reveals the most important benefit contained in the paragraph that follows.

❏ Vary sentence and paragraph length

Although paragraphs may be of intense interest, they may not *look* interesting enough to read if they line up like bricks in a wall.

❏ Use visual devices

Here are some of the options. Most word-processing and DTP software offer you the capability to generate:

Drop caps	Illustrations	Diagrams
Graphs	Histograms	Pie charts
Tables	Columns	Footnotes
Bar-charts	Flashes	Starbursts
Colour	Tinted panels	White space

However, avoid the temptation to go over the top; use these devices sparingly.

❏ For emphasis, use:

bold type, *italics*, <u>underlining</u>, CAPS, SMALL CAPS, colour

Why not experiment with combinations of these attributes? Exploit your WP software: on some systems you find such features as 'large', 'very large' and 'extra large'. For techniques, see Chapter 13; for contact information, see Chapter 15.

❏ Use typography creatively, but not eccentrically
Where typography interferes with clarity, you may lose the ability to be understood. Try to *gain* intelligibility with appropriate typography, and increase your copy's power to *persuade*. Insist on your right to be read!

❏ Don't use too many typefaces, weights and sizes
It can look messy and amateurish.

❏ Make the design look busy, attractive, interesting
As always, tailor the technique to the target. Consumer print often benefits from a busy look, business print from a more clinical look. However, never sacrifice *clarity*.

❏ When using a six-page format, make the most effective use of page 5
Most print uses multiples of four pages. If you haven't enough material to fill eight pages, a six-page gatefold is an economical format. You also avoid the expense of complicated finishing.

❏ Take a sheet of paper. Fold it twice along its width, in the form of a gate.
❏ Number the pages.
❏ Now look at page 5. It should be the one facing you on the right after you turn the front page.

❏ This is the most important page in the whole leaflet. Exploit it fully, by putting your most persuasive copy on it.

Reply element

❏ Make it visible

If you are serious about getting a response, you dare not hide the coupon, reply card, telephone number or whatever device you have decided on.

Call your reader's attention to the reply element in strategic places throughout the design. Consult your art director before you start writing.

❏ Write and design it as a promotion in its own right

If you have decided on a coupon, reply card, fax reply sheet or other detachable reply device, make it pay its way; ensure that it makes a *contribution* to the promotion you are creating:

❏ Give it a headline; put a promise into it.
❏ Give it a short piece of body copy, a payoff and an action line.
❏ Make it look interesting, easy to read and understand.
❏ If possible, include your recipient's full name and address; test this over a split run, to see how it increases the response. Ensure the accuracy of the database information.

Chapter 8

How to Write Effective News Releases

Helping you to communicate with the target audience.

This is not a specialist book on PR, but it is about helping you to communicate with your target audiences.

Therefore, it is sensible to establish a few basics before we start on techniques. If you already know about these, please skip this section. If not, pay close attention.

To create successful press release copy, you need to address your mind to:

❑ Purpose
❑ Format
❑ Content
❑ Style
❑ Final checking.

PURPOSE

Press releases supply news and information.

Target audience is made up of editors and journalists.

Your reason for creating press releases is to supply news and information to those media in which you want it published.

The proper target audience for your PR is not the general public, but editors and journalists. They are the human channels through which you reach your various publics; you must aim to serve their professional needs.

FORMAT

Your copy is bound to compete with material sent in by other

companies. It follows that you must present your copy in an acceptable professional format.

Present copy in an acceptable professional format.

❑ If you want to be noticed, and taken seriously, provide yourself
with PR-viable headed paper.

❑ Use white paper of reasonable quality: A4, 297 mm × 210 mm.

❑ At the head of the paper, identify the contents with a bold, well-
designed heading, such as:

NEWS RELEASE	PRESS INFORMATION
PRESS RELEASE	NEW FROM ...

In selecting a heading, bear in mind that your copy could be going
to television and radio stations, as well as to the press.

❑ Make sure the heading is no more than 50 mm high, otherwise
you waste valuable space.

❑ Leave 40 mm between the heading and the title of your story. The
gap enables the editor to make notes on where and how to use the
story.

❑ Don't clutter the heading with irrelevant information – keep it
simple. All you need is the name of the company, its logo, address,
telephone and fax numbers. Some of this data can appear at the
foot of the page if you like.

❑ A 'catchline' identifies a story, and is the word or short phrase
used when referring to it. Put a catchline in the top left-hand
corner. If your story is about a new range of professional books
published by Kogan Page, your catchline might be simply: 'Kogan
Page books'.

❑ An 'embargo' requests an editor not to publish until a certain date
and time. Use it only if you have a really good reason. Put
'EMBARGO' before your headline, briefly give the reason, and
the date for publication. Editors will usually cooperate, but don't
be surprised if they ignore it; it's not binding.

❑ Create a margin of at least 30 mm at both edges of the paper. The
sub-editor uses this space for typesetting and make-up instructions.

❑ Use double-spacing. Use only one side of each sheet.

❑ Don't indent the first paragraph; indent all the others. Check for
those media on your list that do indent first paragraphs, and

prepare a separate release for them. The aim is not to give the editor unnecessary work.

❏ If your copy is long, use subheads to break it into logical sections; this will make it easier for the editor to read.

❏ If you have to carry copy over to the next page, do not break up a sentence or a paragraph. Don't use a subhead within three lines of the foot of a page.

❏ Number all continuation pages in the top right-hand corner. Put the story's catchline in the top left-hand corner.

❏ Date the release and give it a reference number.

❏ Give a name and telephone number for editors to contact if they want more information or a discussion.

❏ Type 'More follows' at the foot of every page on which your copy is carried over. Type 'Ends' at the end, below the final line of copy.

❏ If there is a lot of technical detail to your story, put it on a separate sheet headed 'Technical information', or 'Technical notes for editors'. This avoids cluttering your story proper, which should be as newsy as possible. In writing up your story for his readers, the editor may include some or all of the technical info. In separating technical info from news, you offer the editor the opportunity to add, rather than delete. It's more positive.

❏ Likewise, instead of cluttering your news with background information on your company or product range, attach an extra sheet headed 'Note to editors', or 'Background information for editors'.

Having firmly established the basics, let's now look at techniques for creating effective press releases.

GUIDELINES

CONTENT

❏ Give your story a title.
❏ Start with a short intro paragraph; condense the whole story into it.
❏ Follow this with the complete story.
❏ Use quotations effectively, but sparingly.
❏ End with contact information.

STYLE

- ❏ Decide on the type of story you are going to write.
- ❏ Apply the W6H technique: What? Who? When? Where? Why? Which? and How'?
- ❏ Plan the length according to the weight of the story.
- ❏ Use language the editor can use.
- ❏ Write tersely, in clear, simple English.
- ❏ Write sentences and paragraphs of reasonable length.
- ❏ Keep to the facts you have selected.
- ❏ Apply emphasis sparingly, and only where it really counts.
- ❏ Use correct spelling and punctuation.
- ❏ Avoid self-praise and exaggeration.

FINAL CHECKING

- ❏ Check spelling, punctuation and grammar.
- ❏ Purge waste words, redundant words and phrases.
- ❏ Check the accuracy of your facts and statements.
- ❏ Read it over for sense and storyline.
- ❏ Make sure your picture and its caption are relevant.

EXPLOITING THESE TECHNIQUES

Content

❏ Give your story a title

Your title should tell the editor at one glance what the story is about. If it looks right for his publication, he may read the whole press release. If not, he will stop right there, and bin it.

Guidelines for titles:

- ❏ Make your title a simple summary of the key point in the story.
- ❏ Sub-eds usually write their own titles. This is inevitably in their publication's own style, designed to tempt its readers. Therefore, don't be witty, waggish or eccentric with your titles; the editorial staff can quite easily do that for themselves. Just stick to the central fact.
- ❏ Your title should be just long enough to cover the key point; twelve words at most. If you really *must* qualify it, or make another point at the head of a story, do it in the form of a sub-title; and keep it short.
- ❏ Whatever your title says, make it *active* by including a verb. 'Kogan Page launches new professional book series' is more

active, and interesting, than 'New professional books from Kogan Page'. The word 'launches' does the work.

❏ Don't despair if, before you start, you can't think of a title for your story. Do it the other way round. By the time you've completed the body copy, you'll have digested the story and be in a better position to create a viable title.

❏ Start with a short intro paragraph; condense the whole story into it

Your first paragraph should be no more than two sentences. In it, you should put the essence of the whole story. The editor can then assess the story without having to read it all.

❏ Use quotations effectively, but sparingly

Quotes add human interest to a story, and give it extra credibility. Therefore:

❏ Make sure what your quoter says is relevant, and actually adds something to your story. Specify the quoter's name.

❏ A quote is a personal statement, so use personal words such as 'I' and 'us' and 'we'.

❏ As always, keep it simple; use plain English, and simple words and phrases.

❏ Self-praise in a quotation can damage a promising story. Avoid smugness, complacency and back-patting.

❏ Keep it short.

❏ End with contact information

At the end of the release, give a name and telephone number for editors to contact if they want more information or a discussion. A discussion could lead to a major article based on your story.

STYLE

❏ Decide on the type of story you are going to write

This can depend on the publications you are sending it to. However, with every story, you need to decide whether it is a consumer story, a product story, an 'event' story, a technical, problem-solving, personality or background information piece. Whatever it is, it needs a core and a lead, and you must decide this at the start, to prevent your copy wandering aimlessly to an unsatisfactory conclusion. The best way of thinking about this is in the form of the W6H formula.

❑ Apply the W6H technique: What? Who? When? Where? Why? Which? and How?

Whatever the range of information in your story, the editor wants to know certain basic facts. He needs these for two reasons:

1. To decide quickly whether your story is a real story, and whether it is worth running.
2. To decide how to run it, and if he needs more information.

You therefore need to plan your story on the W6H formula, so that it includes:

The W6H formula.

1. WHAT: What the story is about; what is happening; what is new about it; what is unique about it.
2. WHO: To whom it is happening; who is making it happen; Who is involved.
3. WHERE: Where the action or event took place, is taking place or will take place. Precise information.
4. WHEN: When it happened, is happening or will happen. Precisely.
5. WHY: Reasons why this has happened, is happening or will happen.
6. WHICH: Which organisations or people are affected by it.
7. HOW: How it is happening; the sequence of events; how people or organisations are affected; how it benefits those affected; how the product works.

While considering this, you need to decide what the main idea of your story is to be. It should, for example, be:

The main idea of the story.

What-led	Why-led
Who-led	Which-led
Where-led	How-led
When-led	

It is unlikely that a single press release will appeal to every publication on your press list. For example:

❑ a personnel magazine appreciates stories about people and companies;
❑ regional newspapers and magazines go for stories about people and companies in their circulation areas;
❑ technical journals look for technical success stories.

Ideally, you should apply W6H to suit each publication getting the story, then tailor the story to match each one. However, this is expensive and time-consuming. It is easier to divide the publications on your list into groups, each representing a common interest, and slant the story for each group.

Study the media you are using – see what appeals to each one, and plan your story accordingly.

❑ Plan the length according to the weight of the story

For example, a story about a stolen cat might just make four lines in your local paper. A national competition for Britain's best-looking kitten, sponsored by a major petfood company, could make half a column in a marketing magazine, a column in a national tabloid newspaper, and a page in a petlover's monthly.

Again, it's a good idea to study the media on your list, and judge what weight and style of stories they most easily accept.

❑ Use language the editor can use

Consumer publications use consumer language; even the technical language they use is pitched at the level of consumers' understanding. However, the editor will appreciate a technical appendix. Technical publications need technical data, but remember that editors want stories they can use, whatever the technicalities. Give editors stories in plain English, and the grinding technical detail in appendix form. Editors know their jobs, and know how to combine the two.

❑ Write tersely, in clear, simple English

As with advertising copy technique, 'terse' does not mean 'short' or 'clipped'. It does mean tight, readable, professional writing. Use simple words and phrases wherever possible. Edit your copy efficiently; purge it of redundant words and phrases.

❏ Write sentences and paragraphs of reasonable length

Aim at one idea per sentence, and no more than two commas. Group related ideas logically in the same paragraph. Make paragraphs of readable length, which do not tax your reader's mind or memory.

❏ Keep to the facts you have selected

If you have selected the right facts for the story, related them to the media you are using, and arranged them in logical order, the story should be easy to write. Don't introduce extra facts unless you first review the story as a whole.

❏ Apply emphasis sparingly, and only where it really counts

An occasional word in italics is fine, if it provides a degree of emphasis in the right place. But avoid dotting them all over your copy. Do not underline words in a press release – this is an instruction to the printer to set in italic type. If you *must* have italics, go to Chapter 10 to see how it's done.

❏ Avoid self-praise and exaggeration

... like the plague. See your copy from the editor's point of view; if you find yourself using a word which he might regard as self-praise, purge it. Otherwise, your copy may fly to the bin.

Do not mention your brand name more than twice throughout the entire text, or your company's name more than once.

❏ Use correct spelling and punctuation

Your best friends are the *Concise Oxford Dictionary*, *Fowler's Modern English Usage*, and *Hart's Rules for Compositors and Readers*. See Chapter 16.

Final checking

❏ Check spelling, punctuation and grammar

Do not make the editor do any of the work you should be doing. He may not have the time, and your release will end in the bin.

❏ Purge waste words, redundant words and phrases

Go through it again for a final edit.

❏ Check the accuracy of your facts and statements

The corporate or brand situation may have changed since you received the brief. A quick check will safely update you.

❏ Read it over for sense and storyline

A final read, and see it from the editor's angle.

❏ Make sure your picture and its caption are relevant

A sensible precaution. The picture should be relevant both to your story and the destination media. For technique, see Chapter 9.

Improving Your Photographs and Illustrations

GUIDELINES

- ❑ Make your publicity pictures active . . .
- ❑ . . . and motivating.
- ❑ Ensure your pictures are effectively captioned.
- ❑ Ensure optimum reproduction.
- ❑ Take steps to avoid problematic or doubtful pictures.

EXPLOITING THESE TECHNIQUES

Make your publicity pictures active

I should be amazed if you had not at some time wondered about a house-journal photograph showing a line of suited executives staring at the camera. Some of them are clutching their genitals; at least one is grimacing in a genuine attempt to smile. You might have asked yourself what they are doing there, what they are illustrating and what prompted the photographer to line them up like that.

Unless you are promoting tailors' dummies, photographs showing people should look alive and active. Preferably, the people in your picture should be *doing* something instead of merely being there. What they are doing should be connected with your brand, or whatever you are promoting.

Photographs should show people looking alive and active.

The essence of this technique – for advertising as well as PR – is making every picture show:

❏ something about to happen; or
❏ something actually happening; or
❏ something that has just happened.

Look at the national press and learn from their picture editors.

What you show must also be topical. A word of caution: cars, buildings and technology tend to date rapidly.

The secret is in the briefing.

The secret is in the briefing – every professional photographer appreciates the support of a competent brief.

For advertising and print, base your briefing on the creative brief and on approved layouts. For PR, base it on your assignment brief and the news element of your press release.

Take the advice of the photographer.

However, don't just hand the photographer a sheaf of papers and hope for the best. To get what you want, and get the best results, *talk* to your photographer. Take his advice.

I can hear you saying: 'What if I'm given a picture taken by a well-meaning amateur, and am obliged to use it?'

❏ *Solution 1:* Consult your photographer; he'll probably crop it efficiently and eliminate the worst bits. Or he may recommend retouching.
❏ *Solution 2:* Crop it carefully yourself. Cropping is the art of trimming a photograph or illustration to make it fit a space, or to get rid of unwanted junk.
❏ *Solution 3:* You may have realised that some problems in marketing life have no solution – this may be one of them. I sympathise.

Make your publicity pictures motivating

Photography is expensive. Make sure every picture and illustration you commission and use has a purpose in the promotion you are creating. It's amazing how many expensive brochures sent to me use photography just for design – rather than for promotion and motivation.

Appeal to the reader's self-interest.

Concentrate on appealing to the reader's self-interest – again, the magic ingredient. What you show should be relevant to what he is buying, as well as what you are promoting. Bear in mind that these motives may not be the same.

Pictures accompanying press releases must appeal to editors as well as their readers. Editors are not interested in advertising photography; they will bin any shot that looks like advertising. Take care.

Ensure your pictures are effectively captioned

In press advertising and brochures, pictures which show something intriguing, yet don't explain, are a turn-off. Turning customers off is definitely not what you want.

In editorial PR, any photograph without a caption invites sudden death at the hands of the editor.

Photoprints

A photograph is referred to as a photoprint, but is commonly called 'a print'.

❑ Type your caption on white paper, and tape it to the back of the print. If you can, tape the caption strip to the back of the photoprint so that it hinges forward. The editor can then look at the copy and the photograph together in the same plane.

Attaching a caption to a photoprint.

❑ Do not use an adhesive label; the editor may want to remove it, edit the copy and mark it up for typesetting. Rather than take the trouble to steam the label off, damaging the print in the process, he may decide not to use it.

❑ Never write on the back of a print. You may damage the photographed side and render it unusable.

❑ Never use staples, pins or paper clips. They damage prints.

Transparencies

❑ 35 mm 'trannies' are usually mounted in white plastic frames. Write a short identifying title on the mount in indelible black marker. Enclose the tranny in a translucent paper sleeve or envelope, and include a full caption on a separate sheet or slip.

Attaching a caption to a transparency.

❑ Larger sizes, such as 120 roll-film (57 mm or 2¼ in square), 6 in × 4 in and 10 in × 8 in are usually not mounted. Mark the translucent sleeve with identifying information, and include a caption sheet. Never use staples.

What to put into captions for PR

❏ Editors look for stories they can print. Make sure your copy accurately describes what is happening in the picture.
❏ Ideally, your picture and caption combination should tell a complete story.
❏ Your caption should not only tell the story, but also help to sell the story to target editors. Put PRO contact information at the end.
❏ Everyone in a group shot should be identified. Make sure your photographer takes the names after shooting each picture. This is particularly important during a meeting or conference; one group can look very like another.

What to put into captions for ads and print
There are two basic styles of caption:

1. the one-liner;
2. the extended caption.

Composing the one-line caption.

The one-liner is probably the most difficult to write – or, rather, it is often extremely difficult to choose what to put into it. Go for the simple description, a single fact or the main consumer benefit.

The copy style of one-liners depends on the effect you want. If you are showing a disposable oil filter for an industrial hydraulic system, you can make the caption benefit-active even if the picture is just a still-life.

Better, of course, is to show a close-up of the filter actually being changed, and caption it with one main benefit. For example:

Filter Mk 2: a clean change in under 30 seconds.

or:

Easy change-over with clean hands: Filter Mk 2.

Composing the extended caption.

An extended caption may be anything up to ten lines; in this case, you need to write it as a mini-story. For example: the problem; how your brand solved it; the satisfactory result. Because this is in short form, and therefore condensed, it must also be plausible.

Be careful not to make your copy too clipped, which can render it hard to assimilate. This is tempting, especially when showing complicated or high-tech equipment.

As always, tailor the technique to the target.

Suggestions for caption content

The content of your captions is as vital as the pictures they illustrate. Therefore, ensure your captions contain:

❑ **Benefits**

Select information your reader wants to see or learn, and which appeal to his self-interest. At the very least, a caption should convey, or strongly imply, the promise of a benefit, solution or pleasure to come.

❑ **Facts**

Make sure you supply useful information. This should start with a description of what is happening in the picture. If you are stuck with a picture in which nothing is happening, refer to something active associated with it.

❑ **Action**

Make sure what is being shown demonstrates an important benefit to be obtained from using your brand.

❑ **Solutions**

If your customers want to see results, show them, describe them. Present them as results arising from the use of your brand.

❑ **Names**

Wherever possible, name the people in the picture. It makes the argument in your body copy more effective. I realise that every machine-minder cannot be named in a shot of a factory floor; give them job titles.

Ensure optimum reproduction

The two main considerations are:

1. whether the picture is for advertising, print or PR;
2. whether it is to be reproduced in black and white or colour.

Pictures for advertising and print

Make sure they are suited to the media in which they appear. You have total control over this, so it is worth taking care. As always, brief your specialist suppliers and take their advice.

The important factors are:

Important factors in choosing pictures for ads and print.

❑ the printing process;
❑ the paper being used;

❏ the appropriate halftone screen;
❏ the contrast and detail you need;
❏ Whether you intend to print copy over or out of the illustration. The general rule is: the typeface and size must be readable. A spindly typeface in a small size prints very badly out of four colours. Poor colour registration can render it totally unreadable.

For more information, see Chapter 13.

Pictures for PR

You have less control over pictures sent to publications – indeed, in most cases, you have none at all. So, concentrate on producing the best possible professional news photography to start with! Amateur efforts should be rejected.

Use the best possible photography for PR.

Point out, tactfully, that although the chairman's wife may be good with a camera, your local press photographer is better. His career and livelihood depend on being better. What's more, he has experienced, professional picture sense; he understands media, editors and print reproduction, and techniques for getting the best out of poor photo-situations.

That should do it.

Black and white prints

Most newspapers use coarse paper called newsprint. The result is that photographs reproduced on newsprint usually turn out poorer in quality than the originals. Therefore, take care when preparing originals for the press, so that your pictures achieve the best impact.

Take care when preparing prints for press.

When briefing your suppliers, make sure they know what's on the media schedule, and have the mechanical information provided by the publisher.

❏ Ensure good contrast in the original photoprint. This is because you will lose some of it both during platemaking and printing. Some magazines use better-quality paper, glossy on the surface. This raises the reproduction quality of your photoprint, but you still need good contrast.
❏ Ideally, B&W photoprints should be 50 per cent larger than they will be when printed. This is known in the trade as 'half up'. Enlarging a photoprint to fit a space always loses quality and sharpness; reducing is much safer.

❏ Brochures and leaflets usually use better quality paper than newspapers and magazines. Next time you are passing a main car dealer, grab a few brochures and examine their quality. The paper, known as 'stock', is excellent. The best of these has a smooth coating, to provide the best possible surface for printing.

Pay careful attention to the photographic illustrations. Usually, these will be made from first-class photoprints and transparencies, with good contrast, brightness and density.

Try to emulate this high standard of quality in the photography you commission for all your company's advertising, editorial and print output – B&W as well as colour.

Colour photography

The best quality for colour printing is obtained from transparencies, rather than photoprints. Unless you have absolutely no choice, always send colour transparencies for editorial work.

Always send colour transparencies for editorial work.

The size of the tranny is not critical, but the larger the better: 35 mm is acceptable, but the image needs to be absolutely pin-sharp; 120 size (57 mm or $2\frac{1}{4}$ in square) is a reasonable compromise; 6 in × 4 in is better, particularly as this size is easier for picture editors to examine.

What to do about problematic or doubtful pictures

Talk to your suppliers: the photographer, retoucher, platemaker, printer. They are your best allies, so explain carefully and take their advice.

Chapter 10

How to Read and Correct Proofs

GUIDELINES

❑ Make sure all pages are present.
❑ Check that all your instructions have been carried out.
❑ Use red ballpoint for marking corrections.
❑ Use the system accepted by the printing and publishing industry.
❑ Mark errors in the text from left to right.
❑ Correspondingly, give corrections in the margin also from left to right.
❑ Ideally, two people working together should read and correct proofs.
❑ Check spelling, punctuation, names and numbers.
❑ Do not confuse the letter 'O' and the numeral '0'.
❑ For large insertions of copy, use a separate sheet.
❑ Check and correct hyphenation and justification.
❑ Check layout, line spacing, widows and orphans.
❑ Familiarise yourself with the British Standard for proof-correcting symbols.

EXPLOITING THESE TECHNIQUES

❑ Make sure all pages are present

This saves time in the long run; there is no point in leaving it to the end of the process. You can lose track of where you stopped reading a proof while waiting for missing pages, and may miss something when you get back to it. Make sure the original copy accompanies the proof, together with the marked–up layout if there is one.

❑ Check that all your instructions have been carried out

If this is not so, contact the printer at once.

❑ Use red ballpoint for marking corrections

Different colours identify where different people have made corrections. Copywriters usually use red; printers mostly use green. There is no hard rule about this, just convention. Clients usually use blood.

❑ Use the system accepted by the printing and publishing industry

There is a British Standard for proof-correcting: BS 5261: Part 2 1976. Copywriters, authors, printers and publishers are recommended to use the symbols in this system.

This is a more or less international standard, because it does not use words to describe corrections to be made. There is a previous standard, BS 1219, if you prefer to use instructions in words; the effect is much the same.

❑ Mark errors in the text from left to right

Be systematic: mark errors in the text as you go along.

❑ Correspondingly, show corrections in the margin also from left to right

Where there is only a single error to be corrected in a line of copy, use the left-hand margin to show what that correction is.

Where there are several corrections in a line, use a right-to-left sequence. If you run out of left-hand margin, use the right-hand one.

❑ Ideally, two people working together should read and correct proofs

Use a reliable colleague; for proofreading, two heads are definitely better than one.

Read the proofed copy out loud; your colleague follows it in the original manuscript, calling out every time you read a mistake. You then mark that correction on the proof.

If you are forced to read proofs on your own, do it slowly and carefully. There's a small problem here: you may have written the copy yourself and know it by heart. You could miss errors. In that case, read the proof upside down; hold the proof upside down, I mean, unless you are really keen to stand on your head when proofreading.

❑ Check spelling, punctuation, names and numbers

The safest method is to read out absolutely everything, including all caps, commas, full stops and hyphens. You need to take care about reading out words in bold, italics and small caps. For example. where a word is in bold, say 'bold', then read the word. Important spaces need to be read out loud, so that the copy-holder can check them.

Take special care over names, spelling them out carefully – telephone numbers as well. Be ruthlessly pedantic; many an advertising account has been lost over an uncorrected phone number.

❏ Do not confuse the letter 'O' and the numeral '0'

Distinguish the letter 'O' and the numeral '0', which you should call 'zero', 'nought' or 'null'.

❏ For large insertions of copy, use a separate sheet

Do not cram lengthy corrections, especially new and omitted copy, into the margins. They will probably be unreadable, and may cause further errors – which you will need to correct and return to the printer.

Use a key letter to identify each copy insertion, and mark the same key on the proof where you want it inserted. Leave no doubt where each piece of new copy goes.

Staple the new copy to the sheet to which it belongs. Do not use paper clips, which are insecure and cause more angst than they are worth.

❏ Check and correct hyphenation and justification

If a word-break at the end of a line looks unsightly, or unacceptable for any other reason, correct it at this stage. Hyphenation is usually done by the typesetter's computer, which cannot discriminate between proper word-breaks and barmy word-breaks. If your typescript does not contain daft word-breaks, you should be entitled to ask your typesetter to correct them without charge if they occur on his proofs.

The *Concise Oxford Dictionary* shows where word-breaks should occur; it's your best friend when proofreading. Keep a copy on your desk and use it. Insist on your right to be read properly.

See Chapter 15 for dictionary information.

❏ Check layout, line spacing, widows and orphans

A widow is a single word carried over onto a subsequent page or column, sitting there in isolation from the rest of its paragraph. This is always undesirable.

An orphan is a single line at the beginning of a paragraph, stuck at the foot of a page, while the rest is on the next page. This is usually undesirable, but not always. If you allow an orphan to live, make sure it is deliberate and not the victim of a proofing error.

❑ Familiarise yourself with the British Standard for proof-correcting symbols
Figure 10.1 provides a selection of proofreading marks. See Chapter 15 for details of the British Standard and the address of the BSI.

PROOF-READING MARKS

CORRECTION REQUIRED	MARK IN THE MARGIN	MARK IN THE COPY	
Insert into copy	New copy, followed by ⼈	⼈	
Insert full-point	⊙⼈	⼈	
Insert comma	⸴⼈	⼈	
Insert semi-colon	⁏⼈	⼈	
Insert colon	⊡⼈	⼈	
Insert single quote-marks	⸲ or ⸲	⼈	
Insert double quote-marks	⸲ or ⸲	⼈	
Delete from copy	ℌ	/	through copy
Delete and close up	ℍ	⌒	through copy
Close up space	⌒	⌒	linking characters
Leave unchanged	✓	....	under copy
End of this correction	/		
Set in caps	≡/	≡	under copy
Set in small caps	=/	=	under copy
Set in itals	⊔/	—	under copy
Set in bold	⌇/	⌇	under copy
Change caps to lower-case	≢/		circle copy
Change to full-point	⊙/	/	through copy
Start new para	⌐/	⌐	
Run copy on	⌇/	⌇	linking copy
Transpose characters	⊐/	⊐	between characters
Indent line	⊏/	⊏	
Centre the copy	⊏⊐/	⊏⊐	round copy
Take over to next line	⊏/	⊏	
Take back from previous line	⊐/	⊐	

Figure 10.1 Proofreading marks.

RAW COPY FOR CORRECTION

Correcting proofs cost monay, These days, changing a single
comma costs you £25 or more; which is downright wicked. So,
it's important to eliminate changes at proof stage - or at
least avoid as many as you can. The proper way to do this is
to get your manuscript read and corrected before submitting it
to the printer. The most efficient technique for reading
proofs is to do it with a reliable colleague. You read the
profed copy out loud; your colleague follows it in the
original manuscript, calling out every time you read a
mistake. You then mark in the corrections on the proof. The
safest method is to read out absolutely everything, including
all caps, commas, full-stops and hyphens You need to take
care about reading out words in bold, italics and small caps.
The most important spaces need to be read out loud, so that
the copy-holder can check them. take special care over **NAMES**,
spelling them out carefully; and telephone numbers as well.
You can't be too pedantic about this. Or, rather, you need to
be ruthlessly pedantic; many an advertising account has been
lost over an uncorrected 'phone number. Distinguish the letter
'O' and the numeral '0', which you should call 'zero',
'nought' or 'null'. Printers are usually very good at checking
proofs. However, one thing you can't rely on is the printer's
computer spell-checker. Like the spell-checker in your own
computer, it cannot distinguish between properly-spelled
words. If you type 'than', for example, but meant really to
type 'then', the computer won't see this as an error. Beware
of americanisms; some typesetting software is not properly
anglicised. If you have no option but to check proofs without
the aid of a friend, read very slowly and carefully. Time is
money when reading proofs; if you don't spend the time, you
may have to spend money instead. And it can cost you more time
as well! because proofs take time to re-set... and you will
have to check them again, to be really safe. Tip: get a copy
of the British Standard on proof-correcting.

As a useful exercise, correct this copy using standard marks. Compare your results with
the next two pages.

HOW MARKS ARE USED IN CORRECTING COPY AND PROOFS

Correcting proofs cost money. These days, changing a single comma costs you £25 or more; which is downright wicked. So, it's important to eliminate changes at proof stage – or at least avoid as many as you can. The proper way to do this is to get your manuscript read and corrected <u>before</u> submitting it to the printer. The most efficient technique for reading proofs is to do it with a reliable colleague. You read the proofed copy out loud; your colleague follows it in the original manuscript, calling out every time you read a mistake. You then mark in the corrections on the proof. The safest method is to read out absolutely everything, including all caps, commas, full-stops and hyphens. You need to take care about reading out words in bold, italics and small caps.

The most important spaces need to be read out loud, so that the copy-holder can check them. take special care over NAMES, spelling them out carefully; and telephone numbers as well. You can't be too pedantic about this. Or, rather, you need to be ruthlessly pedantic; many an advertising account has been lost over an uncorrected 'phone number. Distinguish the letter 'O' and the numeral '0', which you should call 'zero', 'nought' or 'null'. Printers are usually very good at checking proofs. However, one thing you can't rely on is the printer's computer spell-checker. Like the spell-checker in your own computer, it cannot distinguish between properly-spelled words. If you type 'than', for example, but meant really to type 'then', the computer won't see this as an error. Beware of americanisms; some typesetting software is not properly anglicised. If you have no option but to check proofs without the aid of a friend, read very slowly and carefully. Time is money when reading proofs; if you don't spend the time, you may have to spend money instead. And it can cost you more time as well because proofs take time to re-set... and you will have to check them again, to be really safe. Tip: get a copy of the British Standard on proof correcting.

THE CORRECTED PROOF

Correcting proofs cost money, These days, changing a single comma costs you £25 or more; which is downright wicked. So, it's important to eliminate changes at proof stage - or at least avoid as many as you can. The proper way to do this is to get your manuscript read and corrected *before* submitting it to the printer.

The most efficient technique for reading proofs is to do it with a reliable colleague. You read the proofed copy out loud; your colleague follows it in the original manuscript, calling out every time you read a mistake. You then mark the corrections on the proof.

The safest method is to read out absolutely everything, including all caps, commas, full-stops and hyphens. You need to take care about reading out words in bold, italics and small caps. The most important spaces need to be read out loud, so that the copy-holder can check them. Take special care over names, spelling them out carefully; and telephone numbers as well. You need to be ruthlessly pedantic; many an advertising account has been lost over an uncorrected 'phone number. Distinguish the letter 'O' and the numeral '0', which you should call 'zero', 'nought' or 'null'.

Printers are usually very good at checking proofs. However, one thing you can't rely on is the printer's computer spell-checker. Like the spell-checker in your own computer, it cannot distinguish between properly-spelled words. If you type 'than', for example, but really meant to type 'then', the computer won't see this as an error. Beware of Americanisms; some typesetting software is not properly anglicised. If you have no option but to check proofs without the aid of a colleague, read slowly and carefully. Time is money when reading proofs; if you don't spend the time, you may have to spend money instead. And it can cost you more time as well, because proofs take time to re-set... and you will have to check them again, to be really safe.

Tip: get a copy of the **British Standard** on correcting proofs.

Chapter 11
Writing Effective Television Commercials

GUIDELINES

The TV environment

❑ Your message is transient.
❑ Consider the high cost of TV production.
❑ Bear in mind the size of the screen.
❑ Exploit the programme environment.
❑ Don't write detailed, heavily reasoned copy for TV.
❑ Aim for high impact from the start.
❑ Too many scene changes are confusing and distracting.
❑ Don't cram copy into a spot too short for it.
❑ Time your commercial accurately.
❑ Get your script and production cleared.

Creating the commercial

❑ First, write a simple word-picture of the action.
❑ Write the initial script in a simple, two-column format.
❑ Create strong images.
❑ Use high emotional pull.
❑ Start with an attention-grabber.
❑ Try to look unique, sound unique.
❑ Leave a unique, sales-promoting image.
❑ Use movement, colour, sound, demonstration, entertainment, humour.
❑ Exploit television and film techniques.
❑ Situation sketches: work fast within the time available.
❑ Testimonials: use people your target audience can identify with.
❑ Personalities: ensure they are relevant to your product and your proposition.
❑ Jingles: use them to sell your brand.
❑ Titling: synchronise with the action and voice-over.
❑ Make the response you want absolutely clear.
❑ Include a pack-shot.
❑ Allow for a period of silence at each end.
❑ Put ten seconds of freeze-frame at the end.
❑ Liaise with your storyboard artist.

Creating television commercials is a vast subject, and more than adequately covered by specialist books and media.

This chapter will get you started. It outlines some of the conditions in which your commercials will be competing, and offers you techniques for creating sales messages for this exciting and powerful medium.

Outline of the TV environment and creative techniques.

EXPLOITING THESE TECHNIQUES

The TV environment

❑ Your message is transient

Blink twice, and your commercial is over and gone. If your audience misses it, you've wasted your money.

You must *set out* to make maximum impact from the start of the commercial, hold the viewer's attention to the end, and finish with a message so strong that the viewer will remember it at the point of sale.

❑ Consider the high cost of TV production

At today's production prices, it could cost you between £20,000 and £75,000 for each second you are on the screen. Air-time, of course, is extra.

Consider carefully if you *really* need television for your brand, and the budget you need to command if you do. You could use a simple colour slide and a voice-over, but would this do the job as well as a full-blown action commercial? Think well before spending your money.

❑ Bear in mind the size of the screen

The TV screen is a lot smaller than life. If you are old enough to have seen *Ben Hur* at the cinema, and recall the chariot race, you will have experienced an entertainment event much larger than life.

You must aim to exploit the TV screen, small though it is, so that it puts larger-than-life images and ideas into your customers' minds. If you cannot do that, you should try another medium.

❏ Exploit the programme environment

Television is a medium that delivers entertainment, news, educational material and features of specialised interest. When planning a commercial, take into account the programming conditions it will fit into, and the audience viewing it at the time.

Remember that television viewing is a group activity – most people watch it in family groups, and discuss what is on screen, unlike radio, which is a solitary activity. Can you exploit this useful feature of the TV environment?

❏ Don't write detailed, heavily reasoned copy for TV

Because TV messages are fleeting, and arrive on top of one another during an advertising slot, you cannot safely tax your viewer's powers of concentration. Besides, a commercial costs so much to bring to air, you get a really short time for your money. How much should you get into it? Only as much as you can express *simply and persuasively*.

❏ Aim for high impact from the start

Viewers do not watch television just to see commercials. They do not wait with breathless anticipation for yours to come on the screen. Your commercial will be surrounded by entertainment, news, interesting personalities and aggressive, competitive advertising. When you go on screen, go for the jugular.

❏ Too many scene changes are confusing and distracting

In passive viewing, as with TV, the human brain is comparatively slow to interpret what the eye sees. Changing scenes on screen too rapidly tends to confuse the viewer, who may switch off your message mentally. Keep your scene changes to a minimum.

❏ Don't cram copy into a spot too short for it

Normally, you cannot ask for more air-time without giving your media-buyer high blood-pressure. Media budgets are usually fixed in advance. Therefore, when writing a commercial, you should have respect for your media schedule; changing it in your favour can result in a reduction somewhere else. All media scheduling is compromise, but changing it under pressure is bad campaign planning technique.

All media scheduling is compromise.

On the other hand, what can you do if your marketing director wants *everything* put into a single commercial, and it won't fit the scheduled length? Here are some possibilities:

1. Prepare a list of sales points and other elements; arrange them in order of importance.
2. Get your marketing director to agree this list.
3. Write the commercial in this order. Time it.
4. If what you have written goes over the scheduled length, cut out the least important elements from the bottom up, until it fits.
5. Discuss this with your marketing director. Having agreed the original synopsis, it's now up to him to authorise any increase in running time. Instead, he will probably cut the copy to fit the schedule.
6. Argue for shorter commercials, running at higher frequency, each making a major point.

Getting the best out of the compromise.

❏ Time your commercial accurately

Take into account not only each word in your script, but also the pauses between words and phrases. Sound-effects also take up time, and so do the pauses between them.

Don't be tempted to stuff a word or sound into every possible pause; every commercial has its natural pace, and you should strive to achieve this. Pacing takes up time too; be prepared.

❏ Get your script and production cleared

You need to send all completed scripts to the Broadcast Advertising Clearance Centre for vetting. You must submit copies of your finished commercials as well. Why take this trouble? Because no TV station will accept your commercials if you don't get them BACC-approved first.

All scripts must be approved by BACC.

The BACC is your best safeguard against breaching the law, the Broadcasting Act in particular. The new Act came into force at the beginning of 1992, and could well be updated from time to time. If the BACC advises you to amend your scripts, you can be sure it's necessary.

Reasons for BACC approval.

Why must you have the finished commercial checked, as well as the script? Wouldn't it be sufficient to submit just the script, since you are unlikely to put into the video anything not already in the copy?

Suppose you are advertising garden furniture. The commercial is shot in a garden, with adults and children, householder and several guests. They are enjoying a barbecue. Looks innocent enough at script stage. However, one of the guests is holding a prop, a glass of lager; he takes a sip. If any child is in the frame, if any guest is under 25 years – or even looks under 25 – you may be breaching the Code.

Having your material checked by the BACC helps you avoid problems like these.

Creating the commercial

❑ First, write a simple word-picture of the action

You know what you are putting into a commercial, and what is going on in it, but nobody else does. Communicate with your director; put your thoughts into a paragraph. Keep it simple. Just express your intentions. Don't use television technical terminology unless there is no other way of expressing yourself.

For example:

A woman and two children get into a taxi. She asks the driver to go to the nearest supermarket. On the way, they chat about baking for her daughter's birthday party, and the benefits in using Sunshine Margarine. The taxi pulls up outside the supermarket; the woman leaps out, leaving the children with the driver. The voice-over repeats the product benefits at the end.

❑ Write the initial script in a simple, two-column format

This should be a simple description of the spoken copy, if any, and the visual that accompanies it. Do not write it as a shooting script; do not put in any stage directions or other technical instructions. Leave this to the production company.

See the specimen script at the end of this chapter.

❑ Create strong images

If you want your commercial's sales message to be recalled at the point of sale, use images strong enough to do this difficult job. Every advertiser strives to do this; few succeed in linking these images with major sales points. Link your USP (unique selling proposition) with a powerful visual image. Think what this could do for your sales!

❏ Use high emotional pull

When this book is published, there should still be puppies pulling toilet rolls across your TV screen. Mothers may still be taking their young daughters to the dentist, saying 'I felt so guilty!' Babies will still be used to sell insurance, grannies to sell low-calorie meals, pre-teenage pirates to sell fish-fingers. See what I mean? If not, watch commercial TV more closely and critically.

❏ Start with an attention-grabber

Your audience may not be concentrating when your commercial comes on. They may be just about to switch channels. Grab their attention with something so interesting, so startling that they go with you, and stay to the end of your commercial.

A car driving off a roof is one way of doing it; you know the one I mean?

❏ Try to look unique, sound unique

This should be part of your branding policy. Put on your screen an image that can belong only to your brand. It could be something as simple as your house colour. Which computer range is identified with blue? Which dark, fizzy drink is identified with bright red? Or use a prop: which sailor has a short, white beard, wears a nautical cap and sells fish-fingers?

❏ Leave a unique, sales-promoting image

At the end of a commercial, a dog licks its chops after a plateful of meaty chunks. The same dog appears on the label of that brand. What does the advertiser expect dog-owners to do when they see that label on supermarket shelves?

❏ Use movement, colour, sound, demonstration, entertainment, humour

Exploit the unique creative possibilities of television and cinema. Make your brand move in such a way that the targeted viewer makes a decision in its favour. Use movement, colour and sound to achieve the demonstration you could get if your prospect were right in front of you.

David Ogilvy says that you should not mix entertainment and selling. This is true, I think, if the entertainment *obscures* the selling and the branding. Television is an entertainment environment, and your viewer is expecting to be entertained. Can you exploit this opportunity without damaging your objective or message? What do you think?

❏ Exploit television and film techniques

You have a huge library of techniques to call on: live action, conventional animation, computer animation, live action and animation mixed (remember Roger Rabbit?), special effects, black–and–white from end to end, black–and–white mixed with colour, fades, dissolves. The list is growing all the time – see the terminology selection towards the end of this chapter.

❏ Situation sketches: work fast within the time available

You have to perform a minor miracle: set up the situation; sell your brand; convince the viewer; wind up with an action-line ... all in a few seconds. This demands careful planning and terse writing. Be careful not to make it too clipped, or your audience will wonder what has happened and your branding will fly by unnoticed.

❏ Testimonials: use people your audience can identify with

Stick to ordinary, undistinguished people, characteristic of your target audience. They are easier to understand, and to believe.

❏ Personalities: ensure they are relevant to your product and your proposition

A celebrity or presenter should be appropriately selected for his or her speciality: a commercial for cars could benefit from an endorsement by a racing driver, for example.

❏ Jingles: use them to sell your brand

Plan to make them sell, as well as entertain. Use sales points; make them memorable; keep them simple. If you hear your jingle on the lips of children in the street, you know you have achieved success. They are selling for you.

❏ Titling: synchronise with the action and voice-over

Words on screen and different words in the viewer's ear can be confusing. How do people act when they are confused?

❏ Make the response you want absolutely clear

Be specific. To get your viewer to take the action you want, you must leave no doubt what that action is. 'Call our credit-card hotline ...', or 'Call Freephone Kogan Page now ...', 'Send for the illustrated brochure ...' On the other hand, there is usually no need to tell viewers that they can get soap at most supermarkets.

❏ Include a pack-shot
Showing your pack on screen increases the chance of its being identified at the point of sale. This is vital during a launch, or after a label change. Consider using the brand logo and campaign slogan, where appropriate.

❏ Allow for a period of silence at each end
The BACC specifies that: 'The running time of the sound should be less than that of the picture by at least one second, starting not earlier than half a second after picture start and finishing not later than half a second before the end of the picture.'

If you can grope your way through the fog of this statement, you will allow for half a second of mute videotape at the beginning of the commercial. There also should be half a second of silence at the end.

❏ Put ten seconds of freeze-frame at the end
At the end of the action, you should plan for at least ten seconds of mute tape. This means you repeat the final frame 250 times, but put no sound on it. Freezing the action is better than having the actors look as though they have been suddenly struck dumb at the end of your commercial.

The mute over-run allows a particular broadcasting station to extend a commercial break by a few seconds while the others catch up.

You may be grieving that the half-second of silence at the beginning of your commercial is costing you thousands of pounds. However, if your commercial is the final one in a break, you could get an extra ten seconds of free air-time.

See Chapter 15 for details of the BACC and other organisations.

❏ Liaise with your storyboard artist
A storyboard is a series of drawings, each showing an important stage in the commercial. Usually it is presented with the script, copy being pasted below the drawings it relates to.

Figure 11.1 shows an example of a storyboard.

Many creative teams prefer to present their ideas on separate boards. The text is spoken by one of the team as the boards are flipped by the other.

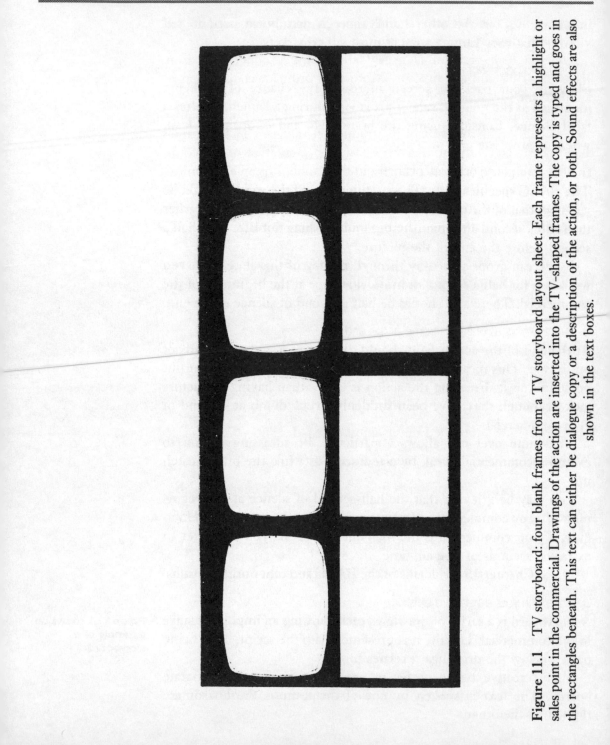

Figure 11.1 TV storyboard: four blank frames from a TV storyboard layout sheet. Each frame represents a highlight or sales point in the commercial. Drawings of the action are inserted into the TV-shaped frames. The copy is typed and goes in the rectangles beneath. This text can either be dialogue copy or a description of the action, or both. Sound effects are also shown in the text boxes.

Sometimes, when there is little speech and much action, the storyboard alone is the presentation.

This stage of creation is nearly always the product of liaison between writer and art director. More than ordinary cooperation is required for this work; it needs to be inspirational.

The whole idea is to show the sequence of key shots in the commercial, and highlight some of its production values. This is cheaper than making an 'animatic' – a very basic representation of the commercial, using artwork and a camera in the studio. It is an economical way of showing the approvers what the commercial will look like.

Eventually, the production team will get the script and storyboard for realisation. That's when the big money starts to roll.

TELEVISION TERMINOLOGY: A SELECTION

Audio   Sound or sound-related instructions.

Caption   Artwork board.

Close-up   Camera instruction: head and shoulders shot.

Cut   Stop shooting; change camera shots.

Dissolve   One shot faded out as another is faded in.

Establishing shot   Long, scene-setting shot.

Exposition   How the viewer is told who or what the characters are.

Exterior sounds   Noises off: traffic, aircraft, etc.

Extreme close-up   Camera instruction: an ear, eyebrow, nostril.

Fade   Picture gradually disappears from screen. Sound gradually fades out.

Fade in   *Video:* picture gradually appears. *Audio:* sound gradually builds up.

Fade up   Same as Fade in.

Fade out   *Video:* picture gradually disappears. *Audio:* sound gradually fades.

Film-clip   Piece of film used as a spliced insert.

Fix   Firmly establish in the viewer's mind.

Flashback   Shot of a previous action.

Format   Style of script or programme.

Frame   What the camera 'sees'.

Freeze-frame   The effect of a still image; a frame repeated.

Go to black   Blank screen in black.

Image   The picture shown on the screen.

Interior sounds   For example, aircraft sound from within the plane.

Key sounds   Sounds indicating a complete environment.

Lap dissolve   A slow dissolve, superimposing two frames.

Lip sync   Voice and lip movements synchronised.

Live   Action shot involving real people.

Location   Any non-studio venue.

Long-shot   A long view as seen from the camera.

Medium close-up   Human figure shot from head to belly-button.

Mid-shot   Human figure, shot head to foot.

Miniature   Scale model used during shooting.

Mix   Slowly fade one picture while fading another in. At one point both are visible.

Narrator   Story-teller.

Opticals   Optical effects: dissolves, fades, wipes, mixes, split screens, etc.

Pan   Move camera from side to side.

SFX   Sound effects.

Slate   Clapper-board, used to mark the film with production details, eg brand name, title, scene, take, date.

Tilt   Move camera up or down.

Voice-over   Words spoken by invisible actor over screen action.

Zoom in   Camera closes in on subject without interrupting the action.

Zoom out   Camera draws away from subject.

TELEVISION COMMERCIAL SCRIPT

Title: 'Taxi'
Product: Sunshine Margarine   **Length:** 60 secs

Vision	Sound
Open on a suburban street. It is raining. A woman and two children emerge from a house just as taxi pulls up. They approach the taxi.	*½ sec silence* *SFX* *Cabbie:* Where to? *Lady:* Supermarket, the High Street.
They get in. Drive off.	*SFX*
Cut to taxi interior.	*Cabbie:* Doing the weekend shopping then? *Lady:* No, I did that this morning. *Cabbie:* What's the hurry? *Lady:* Forgot the Sunshine.
Driver raises eyebrows in an aside to camera.	*Cabbie:* It's pouring. Haven't you noticed? *Lady:* It's Jackie's birthday tomorrow. I've got more baking to do. *Cabbie:* Ah. (*Puzzled*)

Cut variously to taxi struggling through traffic; interiors and exteriors. Intersperse with tense close-ups of all faces.

Cut to taxi clock. It shows 4.45 pm.

Lady: Can't you hurry up? They close at five. We'll miss the Sunshine.

Cabbie: I'm doing my best. What's all this about sunshine then?

Lady: It's in the shop.

Driver raises eyebrows to camera.

Cabbie: She's barmy!

Jackie: Can I have a cassette player for my birthday?

Lady: Shut up.

Taxi pulls up outside supermarket.

Cabbie: What's so special about the sunshine, then?

Woman gets out. She leans into driver's window.

Lady: Sunshine Margarine. It's perfect for baking. The kids love the taste as well.

Cabbie: Eat it on their bread, do they?

Lady: Of course. You ought to know that. Spreads like a dream, straight out of the fridge. Don't go away. I'll be back in a minute.

Cabbie: (*Aside to camera*) They all say that. (*To woman*) Don't be too long, sunshine.

Jackie: I want a cassette player.

The children quarrel silently together.

Cabbie: Shut up or I'll give you one.

Jackie: Thanks, dad.

Pack shot.

Female voice over: Sunshine Margarine. Great taste. Great for baking. Great for kids. Use it straight from the fridge. At your supermarket now.

SFX: Cab horn hoots twice.

Hold for 10-sec freeze, mute.

End

Chapter 12
Writing Effective Radio Commercials

EXPLOITING THESE TECHNIQUES

❑ Write a word picture of your commercial

Aim to give the director a good idea of what the commercial should look like in your listener's mind. Summarise the scenario, action, emphasis and content. It helps him and his team to create what you really want, and get it right first time.

❑ Write a short description of each character

This helps the actors to realise the parts they are playing. Don't forget the voice–over character. If it will help, give each character a name.

❑ Keep copy simple

When you've something really interesting or striking to communicate, the simpler the better. Avoid long, complicated technical arguments and figures. Complications are distracting to the listener's ear and mind, and a strong turn-off.

❑ If possible, use only one voice; two at most
There are few propositions which cannot be sold using just one voice. Sometimes, however, as in domestic situations, your appeal may be aimed at husband and wife together. You may wish one partner to influence the other, or to stimulate discussion, leading to a decision in favour of your brand. The same applies in business advertising – partners and colleagues may be encouraged to talk to and influence each other.

❑ Write true dialogue
Make sure there is a real reason for having a conversation. Then write your copy as true dialogue, rather than a monologue for two voices. It is unconvincing when two actors pretend to be old friends, yet talk as though they had just met for the first time.

❑ Use realistic dialogue
The way your listeners speak may not be the way you do. Study your targets and write for them, not for yourself.

❑ Establish a clear relationship between the characters
When writing to influence business or domestic partners, find out how your targets actually talk to each other. To do a good job, you must express a clear relationship in the minds of your listeners.

❑ Avoid too many scene changes
As with TV commercials, jumping from one location to another can confuse and distract your target audience. You may turn people off before you have convinced them about your brand.

❑ Write a buffer zone at each end
This could be a striking sound effect, a few bars of music, a bit of atmosphere. It helps to separate and protect your copy from the junk around it. Entertainment may be a good environment for your commercial, but you need your listener to switch into your message.

❑ Don't cram your copy into a running time obviously too short for it
When you've finalised your copy, read it aloud using a stopwatch.

That's the proper length. You may have to fight for more air-time. Otherwise, edit it down to the running time shown in the media schedule. Nobody can have it both ways, I'm afraid.

❏ Get the copy cleared by the BACC

Make sure your copy is acceptable for transmission. Get it checked and cleared by the Broadcast Advertising Clearance Centre. You then can be sure it is 'legal', and conforms to the Radio Authority's Code of Advertising Standards and Practice. The procedure takes a little time, but it's better than having to start again because your finished tape has been rejected by a radio station.

See Chapters 15 and 16 for information.

RADIO COMMERCIAL SCRIPT

'Taxi'.   Video Dynamics 1 min 15 secs. 1 March 1994.

SFX: *A busy street. Traffic.*

1st male voice

Taxi ... TAXI! What do I have to do to get some attention round here?

2nd male voice

That's easy. Make a video. You'll get noticed where it counts.

1 MV   Anything's better than waiting here.

2 MV   You should talk to Video Dynamics.

1 MV   Video Dynamics? What can they do for me?

2 MV   They'll make you a video that'll hit your target audiences right between the eyes – and the ears.

1 MV   Target audiences? Such as?

2 MV   Your customers. Your sales force. Your shareholders. Your suppliers.

1 MV   What about my employees?

2 MV	Sure. A dynamic video helps you train them. And it's cost-effective.
1 MV	Can it help my sales force?
2 MV	Of course. How else can you demonstrate a fork-lift truck without actually sending it to a potential customer?
1 MV	I see what you mean. What did you say they're called?
2 MV	Video Dynamics.
SFX:	*Taxi pulling up.*
Driver	Where to, guv?
2 MV	There you are. You've only got to *mention* Video Dynamics to get dynamic results!

(Cut SFX)

3 MV	Call Video Dynamics, the creative video professionals. They'll make sure you hit your targets where it really counts. They're fast, reliable and competitive.
	Call Freefone Video Dynamics – for advice, for help, for a discussion or an information pack. Freefone Video Dynamics. Send for our showreel; you'll soon see how dynamically a video can work for you.

End

Chapter 13
Design Techniques for Press and Print

This is yet another vast subject covered by a huge volume of literature. I have suggested books on design, typography and production in Chapter 16.

Communications technology is changing at high speed.

Bear in mind that communications technology is changing at high speed. You can find yourself out of date in the space of a few months, so do take care to keep yourself informed.

There is also an impressive range of technical journals on the market dealing with these subjects. Some of them, you will be pleased to learn, are controlled–circulation and free of charge. Consult BRAD – see Chapter 16.

Outline of basic techniques.

This chapter does not therefore attempt to cover the whole field of design and typography for marketing communications. It is an outline of techniques you need to get started. It also helps you liaise with art directors, visualisers, designers, publishers and printers.

PREPARE AN EFFECTIVE DESIGN BRIEF

❑ Objectives

Before you brief a designer, be absolutely clear about what you want; all participants must be of one mind. The alternative leads to a waste of time and money.

❑ Scope of job

Establish the basic scope, limitations and facts about the job. This applies equally to press and print assignments.

❏ Checklist

Prepare a checklist covering all eventualities, so that nothing is overlooked. It is prudent to get the whole design assignment briefed-in at the same time.

❏ Flowchart

Work out a flowchart for the job. This should show every stage of the assignment, from the first meeting to the delivery of the finished job. It should show who is involved at each stage of the operation. Remember to allocate time for approval of work. Circulate the chart to everybody involved; there should be no doubt about who does what, and when.

Examples for print and press advertising are given in Figures 13.1 and 13.2.

DESIGN CHECKLIST

❏ Commit everything to writing

This reduces the risk of errors and misunderstandings. Don't rely on your memory, or anyone else's. And don't rely solely on the telephone for giving instructions and making changes. Sooner or later you'll pay a heavy price for breaking these rules.

❏ Job number

This should follow the job from stage to stage, so that budgeting, invoicing and payment are achieved efficiently. If planning, liaison and copywriting have been done by this time, you should already have a job sheet and job number.

❏ Job description

A description of the nature of the job is essential; it should appear at the head of the job sheet.

A tag-line is useful. For example:

'4-page trade folder for Miaou cat-food'

'6-ad consumer campaign for Sunshine Margarine'.

'45-sec commercial for Video Dynamics'

❏ Budget and fees

If a production budget has already been agreed, you can abstract the design element and show it here. If not, you should establish it now. If

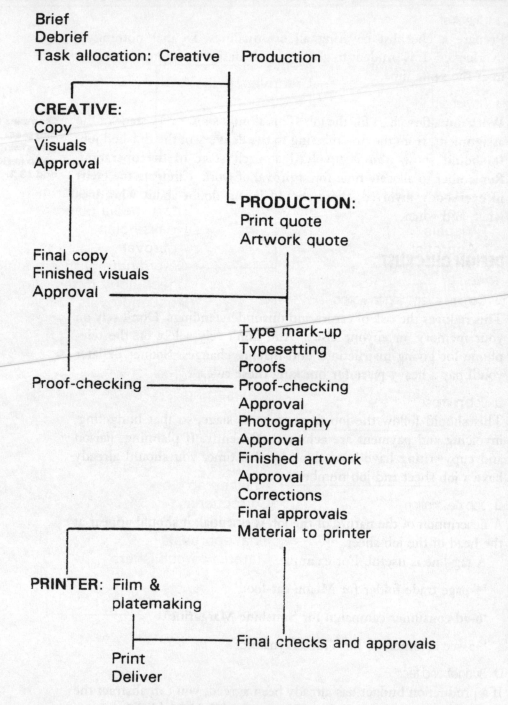

Brief
Debrief
Task allocation: Creative   Production

CREATIVE:
Copy
Visuals
Approval

PRODUCTION:
Print quote
Artwork quote

Final copy
Finished visuals
Approval

Type mark-up
Typesetting
Proofs
Proof-checking ——— Proof-checking
Approval
Photography
Approval
Finished artwork
Approval
Corrections
Final approvals
Material to printer

PRINTER: Film &
platemaking

Final checks and approvals

Print
Deliver

Figure 13.1   Flowchart for print.

Brief
Debrief
Task allocation: Media
                          Creative
                          Production

                                                    MEDIA:
                                                    Media planning
                                                    Media data research
CREATIVE: Draft media plan
Copy   Finalise plan
Visuals   Approval
Approval   Co-ordinate with production
Artwork quote   Check copy dates
Final copy   Final approvals
Finished visuals   Book insertions
Approval

          PRODUCTION: Type mark-up
                           Typesetting
                           Proofs
                           Proof-checking
                           Photography
                           Approvals
                           Finished artwork
                           Corrections
                           Approval
                           Final approvals
                           Material to publishers

Run   Check vouchers

Figure 13.2   Flowchart for press advertising.

the designer is a freelance, agree a fee and show it here. Make allowance for any change in job specification.

❑ Design stages

Decide at the start, if you can, the design stages you need to go through. This saves time and money, and keeps the approvers to pre-set limits of both.

Basic stages of design preparation.

There are four basic stages of design preparation:

1. *Scamps*. Basic sketches on layout paper.
2. *Roughs*. Better quality visuals, but still quite rough in treatment. One-stroke display lettering and greeked-in body copy are good enough for this stage. Mainly for developing ideas and internal decision-making. See Figure 13.5.
3. *Finished roughs*. Good enough to present to the approvers. This means using properly lettered headlines and Letraset 'body type', with illustrations, logos and other elements accurately mounted in place.
4. *Presentation visuals*. For approvers at board level, or those without the imagination to read the copy, look at the finished roughs, and see them as a finished production. Headlines and body copy are typeset; colours are accurate; all elements are accurately mounted. Everything is mounted on board and covered with transparent acetate.

❑ Photography and illustrations

These two items can carve a huge chunk out of your budget. Put either an agreed list of pics and illustrations in here, or agree guidelines for development later.

❑ Printing process

Establish which processes are involved. This is usually determined by the quality of the finished job and length of the print run. Consult designer, production manager and printer at this stage, rather than leave it until the printer is asked to quote.

Ask the printer for a print specification form; this should enable you to give all the information needed for him to advise and estimate.

THE PRINTED PAGE

❑ Paragraphs

Paragraphing is an essential tool. It helps to show the reader that you have come to the end of one stage in your argument, and are about to start another.

Paragraphs are an essential tool to aid comprehension.

Paragraphs help to prevent your copy becoming a wall of words. You cannot force your reader to climb such a wall; he is more likely to avoid reading the copy altogether.

Paragraphs work most effectively when confined to groups of related ideas. When one group comes to an end, start a new paragraph. Where a paragraph you are writing looks like getting too long, try breaking it into two. Word-processing systems make this kind of manipulation quick and simple. Use related ideas as your guide.

When used with subheads and cross-heads, paragraphs help to hold your reader's interest. They encourage your reader to go through your copy with the least effort.

Aim to write paragraphs that are short and easy to read. Don't make them too short, however; it looks scrappy. Short paragraphs are useful for emphasis and dramatic impact. If you are going to use this technique, make sure you do it deliberately. And use it in moderation.

A paragraph can even be a single sentence.

Avoid writing paragraphs of uniform length; the copy will look boring and tedious to read. At worst, uniform paragraphs look like bricks in a wall of words. Why put your readers off before you've put your case?

❑ Sentences

Write copy in sentences of a length that is easy to read. Research shows that, to be readable, a sentence should contain 12–17 words. This is too arbitrary to be a really practical rule, but it is a useful target.

Vary the length of your sentences; it avoids monotony, both in the writing and the reading. If all your sentences are short, it looks messy on the page.

Vary the length of sentences.

Aim for sentences that do not stretch your reader's patience or memory. Do not string out the length so far that, when your reader arrives at the end, he cannot remember how it began.

Short sentences are usually easier to follow and assimilate than long ones. This applies especially when you need to get complex ideas and arguments across.

Rules for writing sentences.

A couple of important rules to follow:

1. Keep to one idea per sentence. If you cram multiple ideas into a single sentence, you create a log-jam in the reader's mind. Your writing then becomes difficult to read. Do not give your reader any unnecessary work to do.
2. If you you've written a sentence containing more than two commas, it's too long. You won't find many in this book.

❑ Subheads and cross-heads

Whether you call them subheads or cross-heads depends where you received your professional training. The difference is marginal.

Objectives in writing subheads.

Whatever you call it, a subhead marks the division between two paragraphs. In writing subheads for press advertisements and print, you should have four objectives:

1. To signal to your reader that another group of ideas is coming up.
2. To entice the reader to continue reading your copy.
3. To signal that what he is about to read is of benefit.
4. To make it easy for the reader to get into the copy at any point he chooses. Breaking up walls of words makes this easier.

Aim for good visual contrast between the subhead and the copy. For example, increase the size and weight of the subhead. Use CAPS, **BOLD CAPS**, *italics*, ***bold italics***. You will find many examples in the pages of this book.

❑ Measures

In printing, a measure is the width of a typeset line, the width of a column of type.

The design of an ad or printed page is usually a compromise. If the measure is too wide, the reader can find himself fruitlessly re-reading lines. If too narrow, he may have to scan back and forth rapidly. Either way makes for difficult reading; both are a turn-off.

Aim for readability when designing.

In designing an ad or a printed page, aim for *readability* above all other considerations. If you want to know what that means to your reader, try it on yourself: what do *you* find reasonable and readable?

❏ Leading

This term comes from former times, when type was set by hand in lead alloy. Compositors would space lines of type with strips of lead.
Points to remember:

❏ Type set without any spacing between the lines is known as 'set solid'.
❏ The thickness of leading between lines is measured in 'points' – another relic of printing history.
❏ The distance from the top of a lower-case 'x' and its foot is called the 'x-height'.
❏ As a coarse rule: The wider the measure, the larger the type, the greater the x-height, the more leading your copy needs.

> **Rule of thumb for leading.**

Copy set to wider measures benefits from larger type.

❏ Justification, indentation

To make your writing easy to read, and avoid the brick-wall effect, consider how your copy looks at the edges. Compare the examples in Figure 13.3.

> **How does your copy look at the edges?**

A copy brick is set absolutely square, with both vertical edges lined up dead straight. This is often the most difficult to read, especially where margins are narrow. The copy often suffers from uneven word-spacing, and much hyphenation down the right-hand edge, where the typesetting system tries to cope with word-breaks.

A viable, more readable alternative is known as 'justified left'. Copy is set with the left edge vertically straight, the right edge somewhat ragged. Word-spacing is normal, and hyphenation kept to a minimum.

Justified-left copy is not favoured by some art directors and typographers. They regard un-square copy as imperfect, untidy. They may also demand perfect bricks, with no short lines at the feet of paragraphs, columns and pages.

Paragraphs which start with a line butted right up to the left edge are considered modern. Indentations, on the other hand, are thought old-fashioned.

Art schools, I fear, seem to know little about marketing.

12pt TIMES ROMAN, SET SOLID, FULLY JUSTIFIED

Setting copy fully justified can produce a number of unwanted effects. Uneven word-breaks can disturb the reader's concentration. Rivulets of white space can meander down pages and columns, diverting your reader's attention from your message. At the ends of lines, hyphens can appear from nowhere, breaking up words in unnatural configurations. A copywriter's nightmare. The end-result can be brick-like. Brick by brick, justified typesetting can build into a wall of words, which the unfortunate reader must climb before he gets to the meaning. Every copywriter knows that no reader is actually compelled to climb the wall; he may easily turn away and read something less daunting. Prevention is better than cure: liaise with your art-director and typographer.

12pt TIMES ROMAN, SET SOLID, JUSTIFIED LEFT, INDENTED

When you are planning a brochure, the total number of pages must be divisible by four. You cannot, therefore, have a 10-page brochure. If you have too much copy for, say, a 16-pager, you just have to go up to 24 pages if you want to preserve the design concept. On the other hand, there are some surprising tricks you can build into dull-looking brochure designs to make them more exciting and motivating. You need an appropriate budget, of course, and a willing marketing manager. Notice how much easier this passage is to read than the brick wall above.

Figure 13.3   Examples of justification and indentation.

**12PT UNIVERS, SET SOLID,
CENTRED**

**Consider introducing a couple of pull-
outs into your next brochure. They
can be made to concertina away from
fixed pages, revealing a range of ideas
and product applications. You can
incorporate slide-out cards, coupled to
elastic bands so that they snap back
into their sleeves. You can have
holograms glued to pages, and holes
to see them through. Blind embossing
is popular, even though you can
hardly read the copy.**

**12pt TIMES ROMAN, WITH 28PT
BOLD RAISED INITIAL**

Nothing improves the look of a page or
column of type like a raised or drop cap. This
is a capital letter several sizes larger than the
rest of the copy. Sometimes it is in the same
typeface, sometimes in another, or in bold. It
shows - with some impact - where a main
section begins. It is an important device to
use when you want to retain control of your
reader's attention. As with all special effects
in typography, use sparingly.

Figure 13.3   Examples of justification and indentation (*cont.*).

Considerations for justification and indentation.

Consider the following suggestions, seen from the reader's point of view rather than the designer's:

❏ An unjustified right edge helps the reader's eye to jump more easily from line to line.
❏ A short line at the end of a paragraph helps the eye to jump the gap to the next.
❏ Indentation helps the eye to get into a paragraph.

My advice: **Insist on your right to be read!**

Typography

Figure 13.4 shows the typeface Times Roman.

Today's typographer has tens of thousands of typefaces to choose from. The main classifications are those with serifs, those without, fancy faces and specially designed faces.

❏ Among the serifed faces are old-style, transitional, modern, egyptian and decorative.
❏ The sans serif faces include grotesques and gothics.
❏ The fancy faces include scripts, graphics and decoratives.
❏ Companies such as Letraset produce vast quantities of specially designed typefaces.

Serifs are tiny 'handles' at the ends of main strokes on type characters. Their effect is to help the reader's eye to group characters, words and phrases together more easily. They are an aid to comprehension.

How people read printed material.

People do not read printed material one character at a time; or even one word at a time. The brain seems to prefer small groups of words. If this were not so, it would take a month to read a newspaper.

Guidelines to help you help your reader.

Aim to help your reader assimilate and comprehend your marketing communications easily and quickly. Here are a few guidelines.

❏ In sizes up to about 12 pt, serifed typefaces are easier to read than sans serif faces.
❏ Sans serif faces are difficult to read in small sizes. They are excellent in display sizes, 18 pt and larger.
❏ To enhance readability, match the typeface to the paper and printing method you are using.
❏ When reversing type – white on a black or coloured background – make sure the type is large enough and heavy enough to be readable.

Times 8pt
Times 9pt
Times 10pt
Times 11pt
Times 12pt

Times 14pt

Times 16pt

Times 18pt

Times 20pt

Times 22pt

Times 24pt

Times 26pt

Times 28pt

Times 36pt

Times 48pt

Times 72pt

Times Roman, surely one of the world's most *legible* typefaces. You can get an incredible number of classified ads on a broadsheet page with this delightful face.

Figure 13.4   An example of a serifed typeface: Times Roman.

❏ Small type sizes on a 4-colour halftone background can spell disaster. Slight variations in registration can destroy legibility.

This, of course, is only the beginning of the process. To increase your skills in design, typography and production, you need organised and structured study. Many colleges hold courses in these subjects; I have given one in Chapter 15.

Chapter 14
Assessing Creative Work

This is a highly practical guide to creative analysis. You apply it to test the viability of creative output.

A practical guide to creative analysis.

Although it was compiled mainly with printed media in mind, you can use it on all marketing communications: broadcast and narrow-cast, press and print, business-to-business and consumer.

It has three important uses:

Three important uses.

1. As a self-test of the viability, accuracy and power of your own creative work.
2. To help you evaluate the work of your colleagues, agency and suppliers.
3. As a weapon to use when your work is under critical scrutiny by superiors and colleagues.

Do not underestimate the power of self-analysis. At this honest, intellectual level, it should be carried out right through the creative process, not just at the end.

This is time well spent, because it can save you much time, labour and heartburn. It can also help you to avoid perfecting the wrong message.

It gives you three important advantages:

Three important advantages.

1. It helps you create the right message, and avoid creating the wrong one.
2. It avoids the frustration of perfecting the wrong message, and therefore . . .
3. It avoids your having to start again.

GUIDELINES

MESSAGE

- ❏ Does it answer the creative brief?
- ❏ Does it progress through AIDA?
- ❏ Is there a promise in the headline? What is it?
- ❏ Is there a consumer benefit in it? What is it?
- ❏ Does it grab attention?
- ❏ What exactly does this?
- ❏ Does it compel the reader into the copy?
- ❏ There should be no doubt about what is on offer.
- ❏ What is the USP?
- ❏ Is it clear and unambiguous?
- ❏ Does it leave a memorable image?
- ❏ Does the copy say too much? Not enough?
- ❏ Is it convincing?
- ❏ Does it appeal to the reader's self-interest?
- ❏ Where exactly in the copy is that appeal?
- ❏ Does it propel the reader towards making a decision in favour of your brand?
- ❏ Does it clearly direct the reader to action?
- ❏ Are the illustrations captioned?
- ❏ Are the branding, and the consumer benefits, easy to recall at the point of sale?
- ❏ Where a sales call will follow the message, does the message create a strong bridge between the two?

STYLE

- ❏ Is the writing terse and to the point?
- ❏ Does the creative technique overshadow the branding?
- ❏ Does it enhance it?
- ❏ Is the creative idea glued firmly to the branding?
- ❏ Does it have a 'big idea'?
- ❏ Does the typography add to the readability of the copy?
- ❏ Or does it make it more difficult?
- ❏ Is it in character with the branding?
- ❏ Is the layout clear or cluttered?
- ❏ Do all illustrations play their full part in the sales process?
- ❏ Are they captioned effectively?
- ❏ Is there a good balance between copy and illustrations, taking full advantage of the medium?

EXPLOITING THESE TECHNIQUES

MESSAGE

- ❏ Does it answer the creative brief?

Go through each point and check the copy against it, especially the research findings. Check also whether any changes in marketing policy or situation have taken place since the brief was raised.

❏ Does it progress through AIDA?

Above all, you need the discipline of AIDA to progress you through to the action you want the target audience to take. It has to be sound to be safe. For the technique, see Chapter 3.

❏ Is there a promise in the headline? What is it?

In an advertisement, where there is no promise or benefit in the headline, what drives the reader to start reading the ad?

On the front of a brochure or leaflet, what *real* reason does the recipient have for picking it up and reading it? What drives him into the interior?

Take a red pen and underline it.

❏ Is there a consumer benefit in it? What is it?

It has to be a specific benefit, with real substance. There has to be a real fact or product feature behind it.

❏ Does it grab attention?

The attention-grabber you have used must reach off the page and grab the reader by the eyeballs. Nothing less will have the impact you need.

❏ What exactly does this?

Words, pictures or both working together?

❏ Does it compel the reader into the copy?

Is the promise strong enough to do this? Is there a stronger promise you could use?

❏ There should be no doubt about what is on offer.

Be honest. If you can't see it, neither can your potential customer. This may ruin your chances of getting the enquiry and making the sale you have banked on.

❏ What is the USP?

Is it the one you decided on in the creative brief? Does it work? It's the brand's unique selling proposition. Underline it in red.

❏ Is it clear and unambiguous?

As with the main offer, your USP must be clear in the mind of your reader. They should be closely linked.

❏ Does it leave a memorable image?

The benefits you offer, and how they are worded, must leave a lasting impression on the reader's mind. This must reach as far as the action you are asking him to take – and beyond: when your salesman makes contact, your copy should already have opened the mental door in your reader's mind.

❏ Does the copy say too much? Not enough?

Have you crammed into your copy absolutely every fact and bene-fit in the brief? This may be cluttering the persuasion in your argument. It may be stretching your reader's patience and powers of concentration. Can you delete some of the less persuasive material and cut the copy to a readable length?

❏ Is it convincing?

Your judgement should tell you. If this is too difficult an exercise, try the copy out on a colleague or associate not involved with the pro-motion.

❏ Does it appeal to the reader's self-interest?

The magic ingredient: is it clear and unambiguous?

❏ Where exactly in the copy is that appeal?

Satisfy yourself. Take a red pen and underline the words and phrases where the reader's self-interest resides.

❏ Does it propel the reader towards making a decision in favour of your brand?

Before action comes decision. Does your copy arouse an irresistible desire to try, examine or discuss your brand or proposition? If not, rewrite it so that it does. Then use the red pen as before.

❏ Does it clearly direct the reader to action?

Many ads ask for action in more than one place in the copy. Nearly all the brochures I have written in the past ten years do that too. Have you injected a call to action on *each spread* of your current brochure, on *each page* of your current leaflet? If not, do it now.

❏ Are the illustrations captioned?

Captions can sell as effectively as headlines. Do yours?
See Chapter 9 for techniques.

❏ Are the branding, and the consumer benefits, easy to recall at the point of sale?

There is usually a time-lapse between viewing a commercial, seeing a press ad, reading a brochure, and reaching out for your brand at the point of sale. Your branding and benefits must be strong enough to do this.

❏ Where a sales call will follow the communication, does the message create a strong bridge between the two?

You must make it easy for the salesman to open his sales pitch without having to explain everything from the beginning. When your copy is a strong foot in the door, your sales force will thank you for it.

Style

❏ Is the writing terse and to the point?

Can you purge redundant words and phrases – those that don't pay their way? If you have begun any leading paragraph with a generalisation, you may have done this to ease yourself into the argument. We all do it from time to time. Edit all such passages so that you start with a *benefit* or a *fact*, one which appeals to your reader's self-interest.

❏ Does the creative technique overshadow the branding?

Clever-clever ideas, illustrations, typography and other creative monstrosities can cause the persuasion in your argument to be rendered invisible. The all-important branding can disappear, swallowed up in the dominating technique.

Take a dispassionate look at the work you have done. Put yourself in the customer's shoes. Does the creative technique you have used work *with* the branding? Then ask yourself . . .

❏ Does it enhance it?

Does the creative technique add significant value to the proposition you have put before the reader?

For example: the range of vacuum cleaners you are promoting is coloured orange. This is its most distinguishing visual feature, so is important at the point of sale. Have you built this into your product branding? Or have you wasted the uniqueness of the idea, ignored it, diluted it, rendered it invisible?

❑ Is the creative idea glued firmly to the branding?

Canon copiers are positioned as problem-solving. The campaign slogan they are currently using claims that if anyone can solve your copying problems, Canon can. The copy, the visuals, and the strapline with its clever alliteration, work in harmony. They create the *total* effect the advertiser needs to get enquiries, demonstrations, trials and sales.

❑ Does it have a 'big idea'?

Volvo recently drove one of its cars off a roof into its back yard. Just before it landed, a huge white bag on the floor inflated and prevented a catastrophe. What product feature was the ad demonstrating? Was the idea big enough? Was it memorable?

❑ Does the typography add to the readability of the copy?

Whatever else it does, typography must ensure that your creative work is *readable*. This applies to ads, mailing shots, brochures, leaflets, posters, packaging, TV and cinema commercials. Everything, in fact, from sky-writing to book-matches.

By all means accept typography which enhances your message, but only if it is part of the message, and makes a real contribution to it.

❑ Or does it make it more difficult?

If you have the slightest doubt about the typography you are presented with, reject it. Do not tolerate eccentric typography.

Insist on your right to be read!

❑ Is it in character with the branding?

Usually, you do not want typography which clashes with your branding. However, you may want contrast, which may enhance its attention value. Whatever you decide, be deliberate about it, and make typography work in harmony with your creative ideas.

❑ Is the layout clear or cluttered?

Every layout you commission must drive the reader to the conclusion you want. The coupon, the Freepost address, the telephone number do the work if you want a response. It doesn't matter much whether your layout is clinically 'clean' or messy-looking – as long as you get a logical flow towards the response element. Be pragmatic.

If there is no response element ... you may have a different problem. Take another look at Chapter 7.

❑ Do all illustrations play their full part in the sales process?

In your press ads, have they been selected to work in harmony with words to get your ideas across, to attract attention; generate interest? Are they benefit-led?

In print, do they punctuate the copy, work in harmony with it? Do they reinforce claims and statements made in it, demonstrate your product, show important user-benefits achieved by using it?

For more on techniques, see Chapter 9.

❑ Are they captioned effectively?

Captions generate high interest, and get high reader attention. Are you using them constructively – to explain what is going on in the illustrations? Are they written to sell your ideas to the customer, to reinforce your claims?

❑ Is there a good balance between copy and illustrations, taking full advantage of the medium?

Do any of the elements dominate at the expense of others? Is the main selling idea or proposition obscured by eccentric typography or bizarre illustrations, or do they work in harmony?

Part 3
Information Sources

Chapter 15

Directory

Clearance of TV and radio commercials:

Broadcast Advertising Clearance Centre (BACC)
200 Gray's Inn Road, London WC1X 8HF
Telephone: 071-843 8000 Fax: 071-843 8158

Independent Television Commission (ITC)
33 Foley Street, London W1P 7LB
Telephone: 071-255 3000 Fax: 071-306 7800

Independent Television Network Centre (ITVNC)
200 Gray's Inn Road, London WC1X 8HF
Telephone: 071-843 8000 Fax: 071-843 8158

The Radio Authority
70 Brompton Road, London SW3 1EY
Telephone 071-581 2888 Fax: 071-823 9113

Association of Independent Radio Companies (AIRC)
46 Westbourne Grove, London W2 5SH
Telephone: 071-727 2646 Fax: 071-229 0352

The Advertising Standards Authority
Brook House, 2–16 Torrington Place, London WC1E 7HN
Telephone: 071-580 5555

The Chartered Institute of Marketing (CIM)
Moor Hall, Cookham, Maidenhead, Berkshire SL6 9QH
Telephone: 0628 524922 Fax: 0628 531382

The British Association of Industrial Editors
3 Locks Yard, High Street, Sevenoaks, Kent YN13 1LT
Telephone: 0732 459331 Fax: 0732 461757

Royal Mail Direct Streamline
Streamline House, Sandy Lane West, Oxford OX4 5ZZ
Telephone: 0865 748768 Fax: 0865 780312

Du Pont (UK) Ltd
Imaging Systems Department
Wedgwood Way, Stevenage, Herts SG1 4QN
Telephone: 0438 734523 Fax: 0438 734522

Letraset UK
195–203 Waterloo Road, London SE1 8XJ
Telephone: 071-928 7551

The London College of Printing
Elephant & Castle, London SE1
Telephone: 071-735 8484

Word-processing software:

Wordperfect United Kingdom
Weybridge Business Park, Addlestone Road, Addlestone, Surrey
KT15 2UU
Telephone: 0932 850500 Fax: 0932 843497

Grammar-checking software:

Reference Software International
25 Bourne Court, Southend Road, Woodford Green, Essex IG8 8HD

The Oxford University Press
Walton Street, Oxford OX2 6DP

The British Standards Institution
Linford Wood, Milton Keynes, Bucks MK14 6LE

The Communications, Advertising and Marketing Education
Foundation
Abford House, 15 Wilton Road, London SW1V 1NJ
Telephone: 071-828 7506

Chapter 16
Essential Reading

Note: Design, production and printing technology is changing fast. Check those texts marked with an asterisk below to see if there has been an update since the edition quoted.

Language
The Concise Oxford Dictionary, Oxford University Press.
Hart's Rules for Compositors and Readers, Oxford University Press.

Design, layout and typography
Campbell, Alastair (1985) *The Designer's Handbook*, Macdonald Orbis, London.*

Production and typography
Bann, David (1986) *The Print Production Handbook*, Macdonald, London.*
Pocket Pal (1988), International Paper Co, Memphis TN 38197, USA.*
The Dupont Series on Print Production and Reprographics (1993), Dupont (UK) Ltd, Stevenage, Herts.

Desktop publishing
Cookman, Brian (1990) *Desktop Design*, Blueprint Publishing, London.

Advertising
Hopkins, Claude (1968), *Scientific Advertising*, MacGibbon & Kee, London.
Ogilvy, David (1983), *Ogilvy on Advertising*, Pan Books, London.

Media
British Rate & Data (monthly), Maclean Hunter Ltd, Barnet, Herts.

Davis, Martyn P. (1992) *The Effective Use of Advertising Media*, (4th edition) Century Business, London.

Proof correcting

British Standard BS 5261: Part 2 1976, *Copy Preparation and Proof Correction – Specification of Typographic Requirements, Marks for Copy Preparation and Proof Correction, Proofing Procedure*, The British Standards Institution.

Codes of practice

The British Code of Advertising Practice, The Advertising Standards Authority.

The ITC Code of Advertising Standards and Practice, Independent Television Commission.

The Radio Authority Code of Advertising Standards and Practice and Programme Sponsorship, The Radio Authority.

Index